Read, have shared and enjoy the rest.

Your Friend
Leo

1/8/97

God Bless You Both.

Leo Carpenter

William and Virginia come alive in this delightful collection!

Carpenter's lyrical verses are music to the ear! In a few brief pages you'll be laughing at William's antics, or perhaps shedding a quiet tear as these simple yet magical story-poems tug at your heartstrings.

So, pull on your boots for some western dancing. Hold on tight for a thrilling toboggan ride to Sandwich Bay. Enjoy a beautiful sunset cruise aboard the yacht *Recess* with William, Virginia and crew — Kitty Kat and Katrina!

The Altonberrys are the wonderful couple down the block, the loving grandparents you never knew, your favorite aunt and uncle.

The Altonberrys Of Sandwich Bay are ... delightful!

THE ALTONBERRYS
OF
SANDWICH BAY

A

Book

THE ALTONBERRYS
OF
SANDWICH BAY

LEO CARPENTER

KARMICHAEL PRESS

Port St. Joe, Florida

Copyright © 1997 Leo Carpenter

Published by Karmichael Press
HC 3, Box 155D, Port St. Joe, Florida 32456
http://www.homtown.com/karmike

This book is a work of imagination. Any similarities
to actual persons or events are purely coincidental.

All rights reserved. No portion of this book may be reproduced
in any form or by any means without the written consent of the
Publisher, excepting brief quotes used in reviews.

First Edition: October 1997
10 9 8 7 6 5 4 3 2 1

Manufactured in the United States of America

Cover and Illustrations by Larry Barnes
Copyright © 1997 Karmichael Press

Library of Congress Catalog Card Number: 97-70438

ISBN 0-9653966-6-5

For my family and friends who listened to what William and Virginia told me to write ... and to Woodie, my lifelong friend, who said, *"A dead man's drawer holds yellowed poems no one saw."*

Acknowledgments

The Muse gave me the writing stuff,
George Mulligan chipped at the diamond in rough,
Georgia Henry provided the stage,
Michael and Karen put it to page....

CONTENTS

1   THE TUNE
> *William heard a little tune, a song within his head,*
> *Would Virginia's free piano sing out the tune instead?*

3   BACK YARD
> *That which is around us tells much of where we've been,*
> *In William Altonberry, the back yard's found a friend.*

4   VIRGINIA'S VISIT
> *By chance they are together, by choice they now are close,*
> *He likes her so very much, she likes him the most.*

5   THE PLUMBER'S HELPER
> *Advice is sometimes offered by a relative or other,*
> *In this case of wrench upon the nut, one turn preferred another.*

7   SUNDAY DRIVE
> *Although certain complications do arrive from time to time,*
> *Simple stated quick solutions bring the journey back on line.*

9   THE WOOD PILE
> *At times the order taken may be not as you intended,*
> *So ask for repetition and a chance to be amended.*

11   THE BEE KEEPER
> *Solutions here, solutions there, the experts lay the plan,*
> *But woman with simplicity supplants the expert — man.*

13   WESTERN DANCING
> *Rhythm and your movement need not be ended by your age,*
> *Dancing and enjoyment could be on the present page.*

15   THE R-A-D-I-O
> *Just a knob for off and on,*
> *To make the music here or gone.*

17   MARY'S MUFFINS
     Was it luck of the Irish which led him to the place,
     Or maybe just the sweet things and the way that sweet things taste?

18   COUNTY FAIR
     Life's a line we're waiting in, make the journey worth the wait,
     Know that occurrences, both good and bad, lie both sides of the gate.

20   THE BIRTHDAY CARD
     What's in a thought is beautiful,
     If in the thought is love.

22   SURPRISE
     William had a secret, a secret of surprise,
     Virginia wet the candles with teardrops from her eyes.

24   WHY NOT?
     A rather informal proposal from a rather informal guy,
     Accepted by Virginia with not a question why.

25   KITTY AND KATRINA
     William would get Virginia, Virginia would get he,
     The cats would live together in a basket comfortably.

26   ANNOUNCEMENT
     No plane would trail across the sky that he and she would wed,
     A picture of a loving pair and just announcement to be read.

27   THE WEDDING
     There was music to accompany life's more serious things,
     Yes I do ... a caught bouquet ... matching wedding rings.

29   HOMEMADE APPLE PIE
     Would the sour taste of apples that waited on the tree,
     Be sweetened with the sugar of one who's neighborly?

31   HALLOWEEN
     The faces looking in the door were frightening or funny,
     The faces looking out the door were cheerful and were sunny.

32   THE COOKIES
     Where does a practice come from, have you stopped to think of that?
     Virginia bought the cookies, and the girls got chitter chat.

34 DEAR FRIEND WILLIAM
       William's lost a fishing friend, Buddy's gone away,
       For Buddy's found companionship from fishing yesterday.

35 WILLIAM, IT'S FOR YOU
       If the food is on the table and the fork is in the hand,
       Then the ring that's on the telephone must be the selling man.

36 THE FBI
       Was it true what he was hearing from the strangers at his right,
       Would he have a lurid story for the FBI tonight?

39 STEVE McQUEEN
       Is it late to change your image when you're seven decades old,
       Should you trust the friendly barber who has something to be sold?

40 A WEIGH OUT
       Be sure the lights are shining before you calculate,
       For the numbers seen are falsified and smack of errant weight.

41 READING AND COOKING
       He and she part company, both attend the book,
       His will stand the hair on end, while hers sings sweets she'll cook.

42 WEDNESDAY'S LADIES TEA — FOOTBALL
       A boys' game while it's simple in the way that it is played,
       Takes upon new meaning when with tea it is portrayed.

44 STRICTLY TABOO
       Hear the ending of a story before you draw conclusions,
       For the sounds which flow through iron gates are rusty with illusions.

46 WILLIAM'S POEM
       Let the poetry you are thinking spill here from your pen,
       Let others read that which you write over and again.

48 THE SUBSTITUTE
       Children move in levels with the cream upon the top,
       But all are soothed by magic and a purple lollipop.

50 JUST OVERNIGHT
       Over the river and through the woods, hugs, hellos, fresh baked goods,
       Dancing feet, sipped sweet libation, sing along, then conversation.

52   MOVING SOUTH
      When you're North and winter is upon you, the South is most inviting,
      For fingers freeze, for noses run, for arctic winds are biting.

54   DAY AFTER CHRISTMAS
      Half the fun is in the getting after giving time is through,
      Then, to figure out with what you've got the things you'll have to do.

56   SKATING
      Skating is exciting, if it's skating that you will,
      But other things are necessary to traverse a back yard hill.

58   THE REFRIGERATOR
      The tools which rest upon the floor are pitted and are old,
      The box in which they will reside no longer can be cold.

60   FLYING SOUTH
      When your feet walk in the water but your mind is walking home,
      You appreciate the lady who'll not let you walk alone.

62   SPANISH MACKEREL
      Make sure the fire is hot enough before you start to bake,
      For fish when raw, for most of us, is impossible to take.

64   ARTHUR'S TREASURE
      Arthur's treasure would reside in Virginia's storage room,
      Beside the peaches she'd preserved and William's dancing broom.

66   MATILDA MORRISEY — SEAT COVERS
      The birds got renovation, and William, bits of leather,
      The chairs which once had pinkness, in blueness sit together.

68   GUEST SPEAKER
      Virginia here to save the day,
      Though she from many miles away.

70   THE RAFFLE
      Recall when you're rewarded the ones who brought the prize,
      And sit them there beside you to share in your surprise.

72   SUMMER COTTAGE
      Perhaps when next you think about some time away from home,
      You'll recollect the comfort in the back yard of your own.

73 SAILING SAILING
      Ride the currents, tides and waves over the bounding main,
      Reverse the point upon the compass, be safely home again.

75 THE WISHING STONE
      A dear and simple message was that which William thought,
      Others have so little of that which I've a lot.

76 PITSY AND PENNY
      Measure where you're going before you start the race,
      There may be consequences if foreign is the place.

78 DR. KUREM
      The pains which enter with us as we climb the doctor's stair,
      Disappear like magic in the doctor's waiting chair.

80 HANDY'S HARDWARE STATION
      The day had brought surprises William never thought,
      Would come from bows and buttons, the things Virginia bought.

82 THE BULKHEAD DOOR
      Adults spend their money and children spend their time,
      The slide presents solution for play and working time.

84 SANDWICH BAY PARADE
      Girls and boys and dignitaries heard the drummer's cadence sound,
      All would march — except for two — who got to ride around.

86 WHEEL WOBBLE
      Once again she thought it out,
      Now two is one and they're about.

87 THE HOUSE OF THE SEVEN GABLES
      Seven peaks of prominence, Gables here, not gone,
      Beneath a central chimney that keeps all seven warm.

88 THE AFTER PARTY
      An invitation taken converted evening's plan,
      Singing, dancing, feasting — as two are one again.

90 THE FRONT WINDOW
      Most men are content to sit around when off upon vacation,
      But some have nervous fingers, with a project their libation.

93 PAPEETE, TAHITI
The plane would leave the terminal with dual destination,
A touchdown on an icy field, then floral vegetation.

95 THE SONG
Virginia was the maestro, conducting as she went,
William he was happy, the kitties were content.

98 TOGETHER
Swarming bees and leaky pipes,
Children's slides and wobbling bikes;
Compatible cats and sailboat races,
Wood for sale and scary faces;
Wedding bells and winter days,
Apple pies and changing ways ...
A year has come, a year has gone,
But what was new is living on....

BY WAY OF INTRODUCTION ...

William Francis Altonberry,
Who admits to seventy-two,
Dabbles now in real estate,
Among other things he'll do....

While Virginia Ellen Fairchild
Continues active in local social sets,
And has won first prize for hybridizing
Ginnie's Violets.

THE TUNE

   William Francis Altonberry, who was musically inclined,
His eyes upon the classified intent within to find
   A piano he might buy, from a little money found,
To place then in his music room, where he could play the sound,
   Of a single music passage which lived within his head,
And to have the keys ring out the sound, which lived within, instead.

   The ad read: *FREE PIANO, if you've the mind to play,*
Just call Virginia Ellen Fairchild in the middle of the day.
   Mr. Altonberry thought, "Good fortune's on the line,
Could be I'll have myself an instrument and never spend a dime."

   "Hello! Is this the party with piano in the ad?
Well ... this is William Altonberry ... who wants the item bad,
   For you see I have this little tune which has a hold on me,
But ... I'm certain your piano could release me ... if it's free."

   It was then the recent widow, instrumental in the ad,
Said, "I see, sir, why you want it and feel you need it bad.
   And if you are a captive of a tune within your mind,
I can visualize my Steinway singing out in time.

   "I'll bet it is a catchy tune ... might you hum it on the phone,
While I will finger proper chords to harmonize your tone?"
   "Delighted!" Mr. Altonberry said, "With certainty my dear!"
He then hummed the song held captive through the phone into her ear.

        She listened to the melody,
        He listened to her play,
          And each was taken by the sound
        Which magnetized that day!

The music flow concluded, now the widow's manner terse,
Asked, "Might I take the tune I've heard and affix poetic verse?"
Mr. Altonberry's exclamation: "It seems a great idea!
But ... I'll call the Bayside Movers and we'll do it over here."

Well ... the conclusion of this melody, I'm leaving up to you,
With the knowledge he was all alone and she was lonely too.
Remember ... she could play piano and he could hum a tune,
And days are so romantic in the summertime in June....

BACK YARD

   Mr. Altonberry's back yard, while not pretentious was not small,
Centered by a sprawling beech — with hedge to form the wall —
   Shaded distant corner, where was placed a goldfish pond,
With wooden bridge to span a brook, to stop and look upon.

   Grayish rocks with greenish moss and shaded flowers grow,
While annuals which love the light, in sunshine row on row.
   A secret spot, the gardener's shed, lies just across the brook,
To hold the tools to work the yard and keep the gardener's book.

   Birds and bees and butterflies, a youngster's swing and slide,
With secret places here and there where children once would hide.
   Where sounds of nature singing play constant in the air,
And Katrina chases woodpile's mouse from here to over there.

   So, if you knock upon the door and think the man's away,
Use the side gate to the back, for though he's busy there today,
   He'll always share a moment to show the place with pride,
The wonder of the back yard which the house and front yard hide.

VIRGINIA'S VISIT

Now William Altonberry, to those in Sandwich Bay,
Though seeming pleasant outward hid a certain inner gray.
For a loved one now departed, had left behind a tear,
William, for so long alone, needed someone dear....

The Widow Fairchild had just arrived at the Altonberry home,
And as was customary, she had driven there alone.
It had become her practice on the alternating day,
To drive from where she lived, to him, seven miles a weaving way.

The creature of a habit, she had baked the night before,
Or would bring along light pastry from Bonnie's Bakery Store.
For each enjoyed a cup of tea and the taste of something sweet,
To season up the stories of the past which they'd repeat.

She'd always toot three times to him as she entered in the drive,
And he would flash the carriage light to convey, "I'm still alive."
He'd greet Virginia with a smile but when the door would close,
The things which they then did and said, only Katrina knows.

It was gratefully apparent around the neighborhood,
William's disposition had improved to mighty good.
For he'd present a cheery smile to all those whom he'd meet,
As they chanced to pass while walking there on William's street.

In fact a radiation from the two upon a walk,
Locked in their togetherness and laughter mixed with talk,
Showed something good was happening — empty's now the past —
For they had found a newness, and what was new would last!

THE PLUMBER'S HELPER

   Just another thing in common is their love of lemon tea,
Hers with lumps of sugar while his is sugar free.
   So while Virginia sets the places, William fills and boils the pot,
And Katrina slips with Kitty Kat to a hidden kitty spot.

   Now William at the kitchen sink with kettle in his hand,
Heard a drip-drop-dripping in the catch-the-water can,
   And cocked his head to listen more acutely to the source,
Which led him to the under sink and hissing pipe of course.
   His thought of tea departed when he saw a puddle there,
And he called off to Virginia that a pipe would take repair.

   Virginia at the table, the cats returned about her feet,
Apportioning a marble cake, sweets to share and eat,
   Cautioned, "William, take the time to put in place a plumber's plan,
Or maybe wait until the morning and call The Other Plumber Man."

   William shrugged his shoulders as he lifted out the wrench,
And left his other tools to rest upon the bench.
   Confident, he the plumber, with back upon the floor,
To place the wrench upon the leak to tighten up some more.
   Yet trouble as he turned the nut, the hissing did increase,
But not deterred, just one more turn, the water flow should cease.

   At this point Virginia left the table, and the cats would slip away,
For felines are uncomfortable when plumbers start to play.
   And Virginia, now observer, from a plumber's point of view,
And she, while not apprenticed, stated certain facts she knew —
   "Bill, there's a proper way to tighten things and there's the other way,"
And she passed this information to the fixer in the spray —
   "Counterclockwise loosens nuts, while clockwise water stops,
So reverse your wrench direction while I wade to get the mops."

He did as she suggested, she as usual was right,
For the dripping came to stopping as the nut would come to tight.
And the kettle came to steeping as the cake was cut to taste,
And the cats assumed positions at their under table place.
And William thanked Virginia for she had saved the day,
For the problem came to closure when he turned the other way.

SUNDAY DRIVE

A bright and early Sunday morn and I atop the hill,
Which runs away from Sandwich Bay towards Parson's Cider Mill.
Here I stopped for just a moment at the roadside viewing place,
To look upon the beauty which the resting travelers face.

Now just by chance as I pulled up, the car in front of me,
Was that of the widow Fairchild with her fast friend Mr. Altonberry.
I supposed they chose to start their day as many locals do,
By stopping here atop Nob Hill and thus enjoy the view.

In a moment Mr. Altonberry left the seat in which he sat,
Walked up to the forward right and said, "Dear, we have a flat."
The widow said, "We'll fix it." He said, "No need, my fair,
You just sit and enjoy the view while I affix the spare."

She said, "I have one in the trunk," as she handed him the keys,
And the transfer of the tires began with William bent of knees.
He knew the turn direction and one by one he dropped,
The lug nuts in the hubcap and I heard each as it stopped.

Two faces now were beaming as exchange was nearly done,
When Altonberry kicked the hub and the nuts rolled on the run.
One by one he counted as they toppled towards the sea,
Propelled by size eleven plus the force of gravity.

Did I detect a simple cuss as Altonberry said,
"Use the phone to call the tow," his face three shades of red.
Here Virginia's resourcefulness came rushing to the fore,
And I knew that higher thinking brought the thought which was in store.

"Dear, take one nut each from the other tires for those now in the bay,
Then here to sit beside me and we'll be on our way."
"Virginia, how did you ever think of that?" "Bill, it's mechanical intuition,
Or ... I just said what I thought you'd say, if you were here in my position."

THE WOOD PILE

It was autumn in New England, which included Sandwich Bay,
Where the leaves were rich with colors and the windy sky was gray.
　The day deserved a jacket and the woolen cap felt good,
And William Altonberry's fireplace called for a store of wood.
　He'd saved a box of starter sticks from projects worked upon,
But needed logs both cut and split, to make the chilling gone.

　1-800-I NEED WOOD, he reached the Tree Top Man,
And ordered one cord of the proper length to meet his heating plan
　From Theresa, newly hired by the Tree Top Man that day,
Who legitimized the order on a pad then slipped away.

　Well ... Tom, who placed the orders, saw the message on the board,
And mistook the one to be six more, thus ordered seven cord,
　From the lumberjack who worked the north, the man who fells the trees,
Who heard the voice upon the line say, "Cords of seven, please."

　However, through the buzzing saws and other sounds between,
The "one" which turned to "seven" now was taken "seventeen."
　Quite an order for delivery, advertised DELIVERED FREE,
With a bill of lading calling for one-thousand dollars, C-O-D.

　So ... on the road for half a day, from north to Sandwich Bay,
To William and Virginia, who had come to rake that day,
　Came a chug-chug-chugging, then a whooshing, then a pop,
And the ground began a shaking and the shaking wouldn't stop.

　Something foreign in the neighborhood? So out the gate to see,
The smoke, the noise, the tremor, to solve the mystery.
　When he read the name, North Cutters, with the logs piled oh so high,
William cried, "That's quite a rig to bring just one cord by!"

The driver then alighted saying, "Seventeen cords of wood,"
The sensation Altonberry feeling — sixteen less than good.
  He said, "Seventeen is not my load, I only asked for one,"
But the driver pulled the handle and the logs rolled on the run.

  The driver said, "One thousand please, Collection-On-Demand,"
As he handed Bill the bill of lading, there within his hand.
  Here Virginia with her calculator, adding up the fee,
Said to William, "Take the load — there's something that I see."

  Thus William gave the man a check, perspiring as it passed,
And said, "Virginia, what did you see? Tell me — tell me fast!"
  She said she'd seen an ad that day, in the local *Sandwich Times*,
Placed there by the Woodsmen, the firm of Gritt and Grimes.

  "The price they quoted for a cord, was a hundred forty-eight,
When multiplied by seventeen, should make your feelings great,
  For the number I arrived at is two-thousand, five-one-six,
We'll just resell all but the cord you ordered in the midst."

  Well ... William smiled as he placed the sign, FIREWOOD FOR YOU
(TO PURCHASE IN THE QUANTITY THAT'S BEST FOR YOU TO DO).
  Now Virginia in her lumber jacket, assigned to stack and count,
While William separated piles to the customers' amount.

  They worked the front yard, side by side, until all the wood was gone,
And counted up the profits they could recreate upon.
  Then William said, "Come next year, let's repeat the same mistake,
And use the profits for a trip ... and pay someone else to rake!"

THE BEE KEEPER

  Virginia stopped and listened, she thought she'd heard a buzz,
And on looking out the front door, determined what it was.
  She saw a line of honey bees and suspected, "There's a comb
Within the hive above the door at the entry of my home."

  She thought, "I'll scan the yellow pages to seek some form of aid,
And put a halt to buzzing bees seen flying on parade.
  First I'll call the local bee man, and then next the men who spray,
And for consolation, William, my friend from Sandwich Bay."

  All three arrived in an hour's time to check the situation,
And to formulate for Fairchild, a droning-down decision.
  Their heads were all together and their thinking all as one,
When they said, "The wall must be torn down if bee removal's done."

  A local builder then was called and told about the plan,
To expose a ten-foot square as proposed by Bee Man Dan.
  Dollar signs were in the air when Bob the Builder said,
"We'll need a permit for the job, so I'll call my brother Fred."

  Well, Fred arrived quite quickly with the building team at tea,
And with just a glance at the paper plans said, "This involves electricity."
  Walking quickly to the phone he dialed Walt the Wire Man,
And invited him to sit in on the bee removal plan.

  It was then Virginia raised her hand and motioned all to stop,
For after listening to the experts she thought her plan was tops.
  Beneath her sink's a can of Raid, in her drawer a single sock,
Then climb up on the ladder as the business people talk.

For the sun had now descended and the bees were in the hive,
As she sprayed the hole and stuffed the sock till nothing there survived.
And she saved herself a fortune, for the worker's estimate,
Had reached a thousand dollars with the work not started yet.

She thanked them all for their concern then poured a second tea,
And they all listened, hand to ear, but not a buzzing bee.
Virginia winked at William, and what the wink implied —
We'll use the money for ourselves and not the bees inside.

WESTERN DANCING

   Mr. Altonberry's secret alone to him was known,
That he would practice something moving, no one else he'd shown.
   It had to do with music and the way that he would dress,
When interacting with a cable show called *Dancing in the West*.

   He'd first seen it on a rainy day when with nothing else to do,
Used his TV clicker looking for a show to view.
   Nature, news and Oprah, he clicked and clicked around,
When his ears were filled with Nashville and the country music sound.

   Now this was not the music he was accustomed to,
But it seemed to lift his spirits and with little else to do,
   He sat and tapped the rhythm using fingers and the toes,
And watched the country dancers in their boots and western clothes.

   Well, the next day found him shopping for some country clothes to wear,
In preparation for the next time the show was on the air.
   He thought it would be enjoyable to join the western song,
And as the dancers danced around for him to dance along.

   He heard the guitars twanging and the fiddle and some more,
Then he stepped into his cowboy suit and danced around the floor.
   And he a rapid learner soon mastered all they taught,
The Square, the Waltz, the Line, the Fox — each one in the lot.

   The dancer longed now for a partner and one would soon arrive,
For the widow Fairchild, unannounced, was entering the drive.
   The music it was blaring, thus Bill heard not the bell,
As Virginia walked into the house to see was William well.

She called out, "Hello, Darling! What's all the noise today?"
But William couldn't hear her, though just a room away,
  And thus was caught there, flushing red, as she walked into the room,
And spied the costumed dancer with his partner — kitchen broom!

Here she began to laughing, and he said, "Care to dance?"
And she replied, "I'd love, to but I've never had the chance
  To learn what you are doing, could you maybe show me how?"
And he said, "Sure, my love Virginia, lesson one is starting now."

Well, I told you Mr. Altonberry learned in little time,
But the widow even quicker learned the others and the Line.
  And now together in their costumes they're dancing twice a week,
Giving lessons to the novices who seek their expertise.

Plus, there's word that there's an agent who's heard about the two,
Who is scheduled for a visit to observe and to review.
  And if the story I am hearing is a story to believe,
You may see the dancers shortly on the station you receive!

Leo Carpenter

THE R-A-D-I-O

   I called to Mr. Altonberry, "How do you find the truck?"
He said, "All in all I find it fine, but there's one thing that I'd chuck."
   I continued on, "What might that be, if I buy one so I'll know?"
And he took the time to spell it out, "R-A-D-I-O."
   "Why, Mr. Altonberry, what's the problem? Is it something in the sound?"
Whereupon he took a breath and proceeded to expound:

   "Two speakers stationed right and left, two hidden in the rear,
VOL for volume switch so passengers might hear,
   Arrows pointing right and left, plus and minus too,
BASS and TREBLE, BALANCE, FADE, orange lights and blue.

   "Buttons numbered one to six, with each a double phase,
To work with AM-FM in a multitude of ways.
   Here a bar to SEEK the sound which you're accustomed to,
Tuners to adjust the TONE and make transmission true.

   "A swinging door receives a cartridge music lovers play,
EJECTOR switch, ADVANCE, REVERSE, what other buttons say.
   A clock in form rectangular, tells the time of day,
Or signifies the station for the driver on his way.

   "And on top of this a manual — fifty pages long!
Which speaks to operation of the buttons for the song,
   To emphasize the features and what the features do,
Technical in language to confound both me and you.

   "I'd be more in tune if my radio had knob for off and on,
And one to turn to stations I prefer to be upon.
   And since the clock's not working, and doesn't tell the time,
I'll view the watch upon my wrist, for me this will be fine."

I said goodbye to Mr. Altonberry and turned as so to go,
And wished him luck with mileage and his R-A-D-I-O.
   He said to me, "I'll learn the way. I'll have another look ...
Or show it to Virginia ... she'll understand the book."

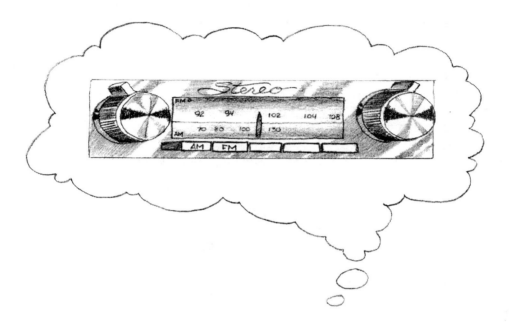

MARY'S MUFFINS

   William took a right off *28*, was there another way,
To circumvent the traffic and arrive at Sandwich Bay?
   But instead of fewer numbers, the cars were tied as one,
And moved along reptilian to the rise of morning sun.

   William sat perplexed, a link within the chain,
Resolving he would never ever come this way again.
   William noticed here a smile upon each friendly face,
Of the drivers at the muffin shop there named as Mary's Place.
   And because then locked there in the line, became intent to see,
What caused this line of traffic to behave untraffically.

   There was no drive-in window, just a lot adjoined the place,
And Mary stood with business eyes behind her muffin case,
   So early in the morning that the muffins were stacked high,
Which necessitated workers walking sideways passing by.

   Corn and bran and cran and blue were the only kinds she'd bake,
And customers would order four — the most allowed to take.
   Then with their cup of coffee to head back to the lot,
Then off for destinations and provide the next a spot.

   Well ... William became addicted to her special brand of blue,
And on traveling days got in the line to purchase two times two.
   He asked her for the recipe, she replied, "The secret's mine,
But if you want some Mary's muffins ... you're the first one in the line!"

COUNTY FAIR

   William and Virginia stood in line outside the gate,
Amidst the teeming tourists and the locals who now wait.
   For most the day is something special, a truly exciting time,
Except by chance the man in front of William in the line.

   From Sandwich Bay down *28*, some miles past Mary's Place,
(Do you remember her with business eyes behind her muffin case?)
   William and Virginia had come in hopes to see,
The moves of Chubby Checker and hear the songs of Brenda Lee.

   William struck a conversation with the gentleman ahead,
"A great day for the county fair!" is what Altonberry said.
   The man replied, "Humph! Good for you, your car is in the lot,
But as for me, it's a house back of the fairgrounds that I've got."

   William said, "That's quite convenient, just a simple walk around,
Finds you entertained by all that's yearly here in town."
   Then the man began a recitation so that all in line would know,
That it's fine to have the fair about but better to see it go:

   "Some anticipate the coming of the fair throughout the year,
But they don't live behind it and hear it through my ear.
   Rockets bursting in the air at eleven in the night,
Traffic there to pin me back and front and left and right.

   "Stories of the horses and the fabled oxen pull,
Sight of monster chicken eggs and 'baa baa three bags full!'
   Sounds of former famed musicians on the breeze each day,
And people parked upon my lawn who come from far away.

"The neon false horizon centered by the Ferris wheel,
Little chicks that cluck away and little pigs that squeal.
  And it seems it's just beginning when they start to take it down,
Why all the work and bother? — four days, it's leaving town!"

Now William at the window said, "Two tickets for us here,"
Then turned to face Virginia and said, "Virginia dear,
  Isn't it odd the county fairs which are other men's delights,
Become for those who neighbor here four days of noisy nights?"

THE BIRTHDAY CARD

   I saw him standing, squinting, with the card held out to read,
For he strained without his spectacles, a visionary need.
   Yet it seemed his arm the proper length to accommodate the eye,
To make the blurs now readable as each went passing by.

   From the rear he looked familiar and as I gathered in the face,
Became aware of Mr. Altonberry, who lived on Seaview Place.
   I walked on up to greet him and said, "Hello, it's me!"
He looked down from six feet or so, saying, "Who else could it be?"

   I asked, "Where's the widow Fairchild?" He replied, "I'm here myself
To pick a card which speaks to her from the birthday greetings shelf.
   Tomorrow comes a milestone, she'll be seven decades old,
Although she looks much younger, that's the age to me she's told.

   "Could you, lad, perhaps assist me ... find a card which helps me say,
Just how much she means to me, how she brightens up my day?"
   I nodded and together we began to scan the rack,
And by chance we found what we thought to be the perfect card in back.

   It was softened at the corners, which showed it had been read,
But then placed back upon the shelf with another picked instead.
   The message seemed intended for the two which it would tie,
And I listened to the words he read, he through misty eye:

> *"I don't know where I'd be today*
> *At the age of seventy-two,*
> *If I didn't have one seventy,*
> *The birthday age of you.*

*"I thank you for the friendship
And the love you freely give,
 And the treasured moments in our days
We now share and live."*

 Mr. Altonberry smiled and said, "No better card than this,
To pass the sentiments I feel from me on to the Miss.
 And tomorrow there'll be ice cream and a cake to blaze away,
So please drop in and help us both to celebrate her day."

SURPRISE!

   The cake was scheduled for delivery from Ed The Baker's Shop,
A one o'clock arrival, buds and candles at its top.
   Banners had been stretched across William's living room,
And pinned upon the walls were every color of balloon.

   A list of friends were secreted from Virginia's address book,
Which she kept atop her calling desk so she'd not have to look,
   When she wished for conversation, to talk of flowers and things,
Just punch the numbers by the name then listen as it rings.

   Virginia was invited out by Veronica that day,
On the premise just the two of them would sit and chat away,
   At the Sandwich Bay Marina where she said the staff would bring,
Birthday cupcakes for the two, and a birthday song they'd sing.

   The ruse had served its purpose, now the crowd's at William's home,
While Virginia and Veronica, celebrating, sat alone,
   And later strolled along the shore where both were bare of feet,
When Veronica said, "Let's go to Bill's and try a backyard seat,
   For it's such a lovely day and I know he'll be impressed,
With your newly colored birthday hair and stunning satin dress."

   Virginia said, "I think you're right, but I'm a little disappointed,
That Bill's not called me on this day and my nose is some disjointed."
   Veronica said, "He just forgot, you know the ways of men,
And he'll probably respond with, 'You say your birthday's when?'"

   With cars upon adjoining streets, Virginia never suspected,
The number here to celebrate the girl who felt rejected.
   But the front door now was open and the scene before her eyes,
Came from Bill and friends and neighbors — *"Surprise! Surprise! Surprise!"*

There were some other secrets and William kept them well,
Not another mortal, excepting two, did William tell.
   For everyone assembled in the yard for cake and tea,
Was taken by a giant box which spoke of mystery.

It was then that William signaled and the birthday song arose,
And there stepped out of the mystery box two who Virginia knows,
   Her eldest daughter Cynthia, her youngest daughter Sue,
Whom Bill had flown from far away to join the party, too.

Then from the back of the birthday box another big surprise,
Seven beaming grandchildren before now misting eyes.
   And in the midst another thing, more than she could take,
Seventy candles blazed upon a five-foot birthday cake!

She said, "William Altonberry, you've taken me too far,
You've given me that I wish for when I wish upon a star.
   And if it gives you comfort, if it brings upon delight,
I'll love you through the seasons, Bill, I'll love you day and night!"

WHY NOT?

Mrs. Virginia Ellen Fairchild-Altonberry, the name it sounded grand,
While William Francis Altonberry, the name he had would stand.
For from a questioning proposal, "Do you think we two should wed,
And live our lives together, or drive back and forth instead?"

Came the elegant acceptance, "Why not? We're found together
Through the hours of our waking days in every kind of weather.
You like the things I bake for you, I love the things you say,
Treasured moments here with you, times when we're away.

"We make such pleasant music and I love the way you sing,
I treasure what you give to me, you love the things I bring.
You've taught me oh so many things, I've helped you now and then,
And rest assured there's no other man with whom life I'd rather spend."

So with the question, "Will you?" and her response, "Why not?"
Hugged each other lovingly and said, "Let's tighten up the knot!"

The next day in the *Sandwich Times* was printed bold and plain:

LOCAL TWO WILL WED ONCE MORE — THEY'LL DO IT ONCE AGAIN!

**William Francis Altonberry and Virginia Ellen Fairchild,
Announce they soon will wed,
For the joys of life together,
And not apart instead!**

They said, "It's time to formalize our swinging singles' run,
And forever more, when spoken of, to be not two but one!"

KITTY AND KATRINA

   The word had carried here and about that Bill and Gin would wed,
It was also common knowledge they'd share the "Bill's home" bed.
   Virginia's house now on the market, at William's they would stay,
As determined by his handiwork and ... because it faced the bay.

   There also was the great back yard, they could turn the extra lot,
Thus accommodate the formal plants that Virginia's garden's got.
   And they'd sat to plan together the things they'd have to store,
For she had one or two of things, and the two he had made four.

   They agreed to keep the 4-by-4 and Virginia's blue Town Car,
His to go four-wheeling and hers to go when far.
   Not a noted controversy as they carried on about,
The things to be collected and the things to be thrown out.

   With guidelines soft as satin, each aware of this and that,
And the only question arising — the Fairchild Kitty Kat.
   For his was she and hers was him, but lest nuptials be delayed,
Arranged to bring his to the vet, thus have Katrina spayed.

   Now everything is settled and the wedding's on the line,
Kitty Kat and Katrina, Gin and Bill are doing fine.
   The cats accept the changes and visits now proclaim,
That just as with the two alone, the cats will rule the same!

ANNOUNCEMENT

   To the friends of Virginia Fairchild and William Altonberry:
Plans are being put in place as the two of them will marry.
   The honeymoon, in planning now, will be a one-month trip
Aboard an ocean liner, the QE II's the ship.

   Mr. Altonberry who resides in Sandwich Bay,
Attended local colleges fifty years the day,
   Virginia, the blushing bride who lives across the town,
Was a graduate cum laude before she settled down.

   William Altonberry, who admits to seventy-two,
Dabbles now in real estate among other things he'll do.
   While Virginia continues active in the local social sets,
And has won first prize for hybridizing Ginnie's Violets.

   The twosome now is active in music and the likes,
They teach country dancing and pedal on their bikes.
   She is fond of baking, he's fond of what she bakes,
And he is into projects and she'll help with what he makes.

   They have so much in common, they share so much in past,
They feel that what is going on is something which will last.
   So they'll put it all together and soon will take the vows,
In the Altonberry backyard 'neath the spreading birch's bows.

   There'll be a fancy orchestra and ties and tails that day,
And guests from in and out of town, both near and far away,
   Will be welcomed there by family to feast and dance about,
And share with all the happiness that a little tune brought out!

THE WEDDING

   My personal invitation had arrived to let me know,
That for William and Virginia the wedding was a go.
   The dress suggested — formal, location — William's yard,
The service written by the pair, the caterer, Picard.
   Pictures by Picasso, the Wedding Photos Man,
With music by The Maestros — Traditional Nuptials Band.

INVITATION

Please come to join the wedding,
1:30 is the time,
Photos taken 2:00 o'clock,
And then reception line.
Dinner of the buffet style,
Seating as you wish,
Your choice of food including,
Chicken, beef or fish.
If you prefer you may come early,
If you wish you may stay late,
Make your entry through the front door,
Or through the garden gate.
Your hosts are William and Virginia,
Last names not the same,
But she'll assume the name of William's —
The Altonberry name.

   The time was nearing service when the preacher, Little Bill,
The eldest son of William from the Church at Parson's Mill,
   Stood beneath the umbrella birch tree of the Altonberry place,
And prepared to join the couple, he in tux and she blue lace.

A hundred in a rainbow listened to the vows,
As the two were wed that September day beneath the birch's boughs.
They were wished the best by everyone who came to celebrate,
The wedding day in Sandwich Bay behind the garden gate.

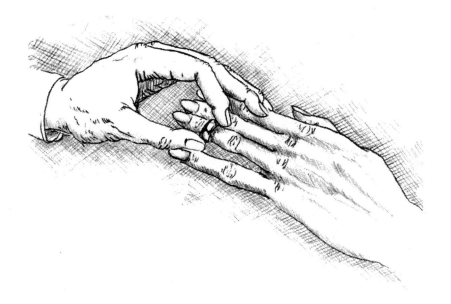

HOMEMADE APPLE PIE

   It was Monday in the backyard, now with leisure time to spend,
William and Virginia chose picking to attend.
   They had watched the apples ripen on the lowest hanging limb,
And watched a greenness redden and they thought of tastes within.
   But with eye to caution, William, plus an apple's acid taste,
Said the fruit was one day's sour ... one day longer tied in place.

   It was Tuesday and Virginia from the swing of apple's tree,
Noticed Monday's apples missing just below the apple's leave.
   And she whistled off to William as she swung her earthward swing,
"I hope that you enjoyed it all as you bit that apple thing!"
   But the mister said, "Another must have picked the orchard's prize,"
And he searched about for footprints with apple-opened eyes.

   It was Wednesday under apple's shade, when mister's magnifier found,
A single silver strand of hair and glove upon the ground,
   And footprints of a lady's style with heels to point the way,
Of William to the wooden fence, with pickets gone astray.
   But the trail stopped at the sidewalk and he cast for other clues,
He'd found the hole ... a strand of hair ... then pointed woman's shoes.

   It was Thursday near the backyard's gate where a figure passing by,
Glanced into the orchard with an apple picker's eye.
   And the mister's steady staring caused the walker's raced retreat,
Hastily with clicking heels across the facing street.
   With the sounds she made then softened upon a neighbor's grass,
Pointed steps were fast and fleeting while William stepped less fast.

It was Friday and the mister and Virginia seemed resigned,
That the bite of sweetened apples must wait a year's long time.
   And William thought of pickets to repair the wooden hole,
And he thought about the apples they had grown which someone stole.
   But he would keep attention to the neighbors passing by,
Alert for guilty actions or suspicious looks they'd hide.

It was Saturday in the hammock hung between adjacent trees,
Where the mister rode above the fence and felt the swinger's breeze,
   When a lady under silver hair and over pointed shoe,
With leather glove upon one hand (while mister's glove made two),
   Rocked the hammock to a stop and said, "I've just come by
To check perchance you'll trade that glove for this homemade apple pie?"

It was Sunday in the backyard where all had been forgiven,
And Virginia and the picker and the mister fingered chicken.
   And the hole was now extended and a gate was put in place,
And the picker had permission for an annual picking date.
   For the pie was oh so tasty and the crust so crisp and sweet —
Besides ... the picker was Edna Wiggins, who lived just across the street!

HALLOWEEN

They had walked the roads since twilight, with parents there in tow,
Up and down the walkways of neighbors whom they know.
   Spiderman, a Jack-O-Lantern, a Casper Friendly Ghost,
All together — *"Trick or Treat!"* — who will get the most?

Costumed conversation cuts through October's air,
Chips and candied apples, bags with sweets to spare.
   Now in a row, now up the street, now ring another bell,
"Trick or Treat!" — with hands held out — is what the tricksters yell!

Tramping feet through fallen leaves, disguises in a line,
Here's a doorway brightly lit, a children's welcome sign!
   WILLIAM & VIRGINIA — THE ALTONBERRY PLACE
So ring the bell, now once, then twice, and stand with scary face.

The baggy ghost (he's little Bob) said, *"Boo!"* to Mr. Bill,
As Jack-O-Lantern (Jamie) held out her bag to fill.
   Spiderman (it's Richie), his cape spread asked, "Where's mine?"
Then in unison came, "Thank you!" as the three reversed the line.

William and Virginia watched the children down the walk,
And waved out to the mothers and the fathers in the dark.
   And Virginia said to William, "Candy's not too much to pay,
To see such happy children on Halloween today."

And William said, "You're right my dear and there's another benefit,
If candy stayed here in this house then I'd have eaten it.
   And what with all the calories and the other this and that,
What will be children's energy would have been William's fat!"

THE COOKIES

   She was reading, he was writing, the cats raced 'cross the floor,
Hers was Chaucer, his were memories, the cats' ball from the store.
   She was smiling, he was pensive, the cats would roll and spring,
All would stop and heads would rise as the chime at the door would sing.

   Bill got up and said, "Who's this, whose action brings the chime?"
While the cats sprung toward the ringer, not wasting any time.
   Virginia marked the place she'd read, now book beside the chair,
Watched William rise and fingers comb metallic silver hair.

   Together as they always were, now with the second chime in air,
He in back and she in front, they walked to see who's there.
   The door now opened and two in uniform stood hesitant about,
Then just as in rehearsal the two did sing-song out:

   "Hello there Mr. Altonberry, hello there Mrs., too,
Hello Kitty and Katrina!" as they skidded into view.
   "I guess you know the time of year from the boxes which we hold,
It's time to bring the cookies which a month ago were sold."

   Mr. Altonberry chuckled and asked the girls to step inside,
While Kitty and Katrina ran aback the couch to hide.
   "We'll have some punch and cookies to see if they're the rage,
The same as those sold by Virginia, when she was of Girl Scouts' age."

   They asked, "Were there Girl Scouts that many years ago?"
As they read the time lines in her face which seven decades show.
   Virginia said, "Most assuredly! In 1912, you see,
Juliette Low formed the Girl Guides, for girls' activity.

"Observe! I'm in your cookies now and was into cookies then,
For our Guides would yearly bake and sell to help support our den.
   So, I don't know if we started it — maybe others did it too —
But I rang bells and drank some punch just as you girls now do."

   The girls smiled and said, "We must leave now to get delivery done,
And we're delighted you were on our list delivered number one,
   For now at every other stop we'll say along the way,
It's because of Mrs. Altonberry that you're getting these today!"

DEAR FRIEND WILLIAM

This pen within my hand has words which it must share,
And lest others reach you earlier and harm beyond repair
This friendship we have fostered (how many is the year?),
I must inform you of an incident before detractors do appear.

Bill, in our conversations which have tied us time and time,
I'm sure I've mentioned Sybil — a growing friend of mine.
Well ... the aftereffects of an injury she suffered has brought upon
Flowers, gifts, and reminiscing which have continued on and on.

So, while my original intention was to simply see her through,
The accident — a shattered leg — now breaks a heart or two.
For there has emerged a younger man who walks a different line,
With thoughts within this writer thirty years of now past time.

While wrestling with the consequences, knowing some will suffer pain,
I must travel paths walked earlier where was played the passion game.
So, Bill, my mind selects a heading and I pray the course is right,
For my heart has shaken years aside, for Sybil, my delight.

Know, my friend, you'll hear from me as we travel day to day,
Kindly let me know your feelings and what your feelings say.
Remember all the joy I feel that you now share your love and home,
Please think none the less of Buddy, who walks apart ... but not alone.

Your Friend,

Buddy

WILLIAM, IT'S FOR YOU

"Hello!"

"Hello! Mr. Altonberry? How are you today?
Let me tell you you're a lucky one, as you'll learn from what I say.
You see, you've been selected from a most important list,
People who know quality, and people who insist,
On availing themselves of the finest which we offer through our plan,
To improve the life and living of today's important man.

"Now let me state this instant that you'll get something free,
If you will just consider listening here to me ...

"You ask me what I'm selling? Well you know it must be good,
As I got your name from others in your very neighborhood.
And while I'm on the subject ... are there others you can name?
I'll give them what I'll give to you — the Home Improvement Game!

"You say your dinner's getting cold? You're tired? It's a trick?
You don't need new siding? Don't hang up, please! — *CLICK!*

"Hello? ... Mr. Altonberry? ... Hello?"

THE FBI

   Virginia at the pharmacy attends the aging aisle,
Bluing for the graying hair, lipstick for her smile.
   William on the sidewalk of the Mid-Town Mini Mall,
Read an advertisement pasted new upon the wall:

   YOSHI'S JAPANESE PARLOR WITH SUSHI THAT'S THE BEST
OR BUFFET LINE WITH DEEP FRIED TREATS — THE ORIENT EXPRESS

   William searching memory recalled his Eastern stay,
And his pallet recollected having curried rice one day.
   The scent of Yoshi's specials and an oriental song,
Brought William to the doorknob and the hostess Shi Shu Wong.

   William was directed where the shoeless patrons sit,
To the floor with six-inch tables and the incense candles lit.
   He bowed and placed his order as he settled to the floor,
"I'll have curried rice, chicken strips, green tea and no more."

   Everyone was smiling showing oriental white,
Except two shaded gentlemen closely seated to his right.
   One cast an air of mystery as he searched the place about,
While the other placed a package on the table, then walked out.
   In an instant came another man of suspicious searching eye,
Who took his seat upon the floor by the mysterious mustachioed guy.

   William sipped upon his tea and practiced with his sticks,
He drummed upon the little dish and performed some music tricks.
   Soon Shi Shu Wong brought silver and placed it at his right,
And with accented English commented, "Best you use these things tonight."

William's tapping hung in air as the whispers to his right,
Now accompanied by crackling sounds of undone package tight.
   And the guys gazed in the parcel and the volume was increased,
And the mustache spoke mysterious, "This trafficking must cease.
   This sample of the product you expect those here to buy,
Will certainly be confiscated by the local FBI."

William bent a little closer to this moment of intrigue,
His fork within the curried rice, soy sauce stained his sleeve.
   He would certainly have a story for Virginia for the ride!
Were they agents? Were they buyers? What was their party side?

The mustache buried in the box was sniffing and was feeling,
And William listened harder for the facts they were concealing.
   He heard, "This box, if representative of the shipload we'll receive,
Is of a lesser quality surely than the corporate men believe.
   And you, I and the deliverer will stand before the Director's seat,
With none to sell or distribute ... all alone ours to eat!

Beads of sweat now gathered, what had William heard?
Was he upon a secret, a legal bending word?
   He recorded all the details on his information pad,
Here was William the detective with a story to be had!
   Squashed and slippery ... yellow to the core ...
Spotted and discolored ... move it quick when less is more.

The curried rice was cold now and the green tea chilled his cup,
And the strangers put on their coats as they struggled to stand up.
   They left the package lying with the notes which they had written,
And William stretched to read them from the spot where he was sitting.
   He crumpled up the notes he took and closed suspicious eye,
Now aware Florida Banana Incorporated was not the FBI!

With William at the car door and Virginia in her seat,
She listened to the story of Bill's oriental treat.
   William's face was blushing as Virginia's lips spoke true,
"William, when you're hungry, take me along with you!

"For you know I see things differently as my insight's more acute,
I know letters such as F-B-I don't smack of ill repute.
   For Federal's far from Florida, and Bureau's not a bunch,
And bananas slipping across state lines are not investigative's my hunch!"

STEVE MCQUEEN

William now within the barber shop and settled in the chair,
No need for explanation of the reason he was there.
  With tresses now unruly there was some that he could spare,
It was time to get a styling, it was time to shape the hair.

Angelo the barber now entered on the scene,
And noted that the visitor in leather coat and jeans,
  While looking some familiar caused his hair to stand on end,
And he hoped that just a cutting did the visitor intend.

He stepped to face the stranger and to look him in the eye,
Then make his time worn comment, "It's *a* nice *a* you come by!"
  Relieved now with frontal observation, the stranger proved to be,
None other than his *a* once *a* month *a* customer — Bill Alton*a*berry.

"Hey, you fool *a* me Bill! Why you dress *a* like that,
Why you look *a* so mean and *a* lean?"
  And Bill replied, "I've just come by
For the look of Steve McQueen.
  This morning on a special they showed that all around the world
They're trying for Steve's short-hair look — flat without the curl."

"I'm *a* the guy that *a* cuts *a* the hair, you're *a* the guy that's in *a* the chair,
But the hair on *a* the floor will never *a* grow on your head *a* no more!"
  And what of Virginia? What will *a* she say,
When *a* you come home *a* looking so young *a* today?"

Here Bill gave his assurance, "She's given her consent,
As with every other thing I do, you know that she's content.
  Be not concerned about Virginia, she too was taken by what we saw,
In fact, is presently under Ramona's scissors for the look of Ali McGraw!"

A WEIGH OUT

Was the whistle heard by William from Virginia on the scale —
A twill which went from low to high then back to low the trail —
A sound to voice displeasure as the wheel of numbers spun,
Suggesting to her upon the scale there's something to be done?

Virginia cried, "Dear William, something here's gone wrong!
The numbers of the weigher present a gainer's song.
You know it's my displeasure a variance of weight,
So be prepared our mealtime fare will show a different plate."

William said, "Now just a minute Dear, what brings on your conclusion
That your weight is up? You look just fine, the scale presents illusion!"
She said, "The numbers there upon the wheel envisioned spinning by,
Present the picture one-four-three and pictures never lie.

"Come here dear William, see yourself what brings my spirit down,
No woman lives contented here who gains an extra pound.
Thus my intention Dearest, despite what you might feel,
Is for us to exercise and chew upon leaner meal."

William, at her shoulder now, saw the numbers in her sight,
And indeed the number she had uttered — one-four-three — was right.
But between her furry slippers a passenger there sat,
In fact ten pounds of Katrina's friend — you remember Kitty Kat?

Bill commanded, "Off of there!" and Kitty scat in flight,
Which brought the scale to one-three-three, and to Virginia — delight!
William saw a smile emerge and he was smiling too,
Funny what the rapid loss of ten pounds there did do!

READING AND COOKING

William lies on the sofa with his library book,
Virginia with hers in the kitchen to cook.

His with intriguing mysterious lines,
Hers of sweetness, of frosting the kind.

He in the middle of murder and such,
She in the shelling and crushing of nuts.

He touched by the hero engaged in the chase,
She fingers the line of her recipe place.

He skips to the ending past quickly turned pages,
She apportions the powders and sugars and sages.

He warms from the cats who sit 'side his lap,
She cools down the mix from the cold water tap.

He walks to the window and is bathed in the light,
She shuts oven's door on the recipe tight.

He closes the book for his reading is done,
She opens the oven at a quarter to one.

He sits at the table and points out the plot,
She pours him some tea and serves gingerbread hot.

WEDNESDAY'S LADIES TEA — FOOTBALL

Virginia watched the football game beneath a blanket there with Bill,
For next day at the Ladies Tea a speaker's slot she'd fill.
And while her usual talk was flowers or a recent book she'd read,
The Wednesday dissertation would be the football game instead.

When asked if she would expound upon exactly what she'd seen,
While sitting on the fifty above the Bayside Football Team,
She replied, "Why certainly," and commenced to then unfold,
The finer points of football through this muddled message told:

"There were eleven scattered members, eleven in a line,
Separate and distinctive colors, to visually define.
Five older men positioned, striped in white and black,
With whistles hanging round the neck and yellowed pockets back.

"The clock is placed at zero, a hand waves in the air,
A whistle blows and the kicker knows it's time the ball's to air.
One of the scattered members awaits to catch the ball,
And the other ten, who are dressed like him, drop back to form a wall.

"The sides rush at each other and are piled up on the field,
With the catcher on the bottom and the ball he caught concealed.
A striper yells, 'First and ten!' And the crowd yells, 'Hold that line!'
With the bodies on the other side screaming, 'Pass the ball this time!'

"The boys who wear the colors pile up once again,
And are separated by the referees, who are the older men.
Another in a striped suit puts the ball down on the line,
And calls to those on either side, 'Play ball ... second and nine!'

"Then 'third and eight' and 'fourth and kick,' the sides exchange the ball,
And the line becomes the scattered and the scattered form the wall.
   At halftime came the marching bands, again the whistle blew,
And the roar came from the stands to say what each team now must do.

   "So, they ran and threw and pushed and rolled, four quarters of the game,
And mud and grass and conflict turned colors all the same.
   Now uniforms a muddy blur and players seem as one,
Who knock each other to the ground until the game is done.

   "So on and on — one hour's time — the battle did ensue,
Before a gunshot filled the air to express the game as through.
   And the players, bruised and tired, slipped beneath the stands,
To the strains of *Hail the Heroes* played by the football bands."

   The applause she got was deafening, the sport was clarified,
And the girls would join their husbands for the weekly football ride,
   To sit in stands beside them and cheer the hometown's name,
For surely now they understood the nuances of the game!

STRICTLY TABOO

    The wind was but a whisper as leaves traced to the ground,
And the moon was round and silver and the night was free of sound.
    The sun had rolled the corner, now the chimes sang six o'clock,
And William and Virginia stepped on mid November's walk.

    They now beyond elegance of the Dunston Barry Estate,
Encompassed there by fieldstone wall and iron lioned gate,
    Were frozen by a woman's shout, their step was locked surprise,
As twilight set upon the sound and evening shaded eyes.

    "What was that piercing dissonance which rattled down my back,
And caused this shake and shiver, my steps stopped in their track?"
    Then William on the inside near the bars upon the gate,
Said, "It sounded like, *'That's TABOO my dear — I'm forty-six, you're twenty-eight!'*
    It's mighty strange a call like that within this neighborhood,
Where all is prim and proper, above the board and seeming good."

    Without a word the Altonberrys turned eyes to face the bars,
And looked in on the inner yard aligned with fancy cars.
    They caught the smell of sausage and sensed argumentative sound,
And Dunston Barry's voice rang out, "I'll beat you good this round!
    Sharpened knife, a gun, a club, a rap upon the head!"
The retort was, "Sorry Dunston! Time is up! Your chance to win's abed!"

    The Neighborhood Uniformed Patrol, by chance around the bay,
Heard William giving whistle and with siren sped their way.
    William explained the occurrences and the sounds which they had heard,
Which prompted official attention: "Mr. Barry — please, a word."
    Dunston Barry and his lady then approached them unabated,
And the officer mirrored the story that William had related.

Here Lady Dunston Barry and Dunston Barry too,
Said, "The sounds were misinterpreted, just a game was played, *TABOO!*
And though the contest was spirited and sounds interpreted, severe,
It was only friends and neighbors in a party atmosphere.
In fact a couple's leaving and two seats could take a pair,
Would the strangers who were so concerned care to join the party fare?"

William checked Virginia and Virginia checked the time,
And they sensed a competition, in which they revel, on the line.
The cats had had their evening meal, papers had been read,
And once around the block could be a gaming time instead.
So the Dunston Barrys introduced, "The Altonberrys here,
Have come to eat some sausage and assume a *TABOO* chair!"

WILLIAM'S POEM

Virginia heard his laughter tumble down the attic's stair,
And asked the question, "William, what's so funny in the air?"
 He responded, "Come and see this, it's a poem with a date,
And should my calculation be correct, my writing age was eight."

Virginia, quick with numbers, but quicker on her feet,
Now up the stairs beside him with a cardboard box the seat,
 Said, "Your calculation's very close but not the same as mine,
For the date that's on the laughing matter puts your age at nine.

"Why don't you read it to me Bill, and let me share the laugh?
Or you begin the reading and I'll read the second half."
 Bill said, "No, I'll read it all while you just concentrate,
But remember when I wrote it, I'd just turned nine from eight.

"I recall the teacher saying, 'Glorify the year,
And talk about the things which come about both home and here.
 Talk about the holidays, the weather and the time,
And I'll give you extra credit if you make the whole thing rhyme!'

"I further recall the handing in of the assignment on that day,
And watching Mrs. Tinkle's tresses turn a bit more gray
 As she called out, 'William Altonberry, is this a writing or a joke?'
I said, 'It's a rhymer Mrs. Tinkle, my poetic voice just spoke.'

"She said, 'Come forward then and read it, stand before your mates,
The other children in the class, the other nines and eights.'
 So I walked and took my poem and held it out to read
Aloud then to the children to see if they agreed:

"'Thirty days hath September,
Halloween and then November,
 Nuts and berries, turkey too,
Santa Claus, December's through.

'January's mighty cold,
Second month and winter's old,
 March wind whistles, empty trees,
April fools first warm day's bees.

'May a bud, a flower too,
Collect the books,
 It's June —
We're through!'"

Bill commenced to laughing, with Virginia rolling too,
She caught her breath and said, "Delightful! Goody-good for you!"
 He said, "That's the way the children saw it as they wriggled in their seats,
But quiet came when Tinkle said, 'No recess time nor treats!

'And as for you, my William, put this rhyme away somewhere,
And someday when you're more mature, read it from your chair.
 And ask yourself the question then, was this the proper time,
To submit to Mrs. Tinkle this Altonberry rhyme?'"

Then William said, "God rest her soul wherever she may be,
For the words have brought a second laugh to Virginia and to me.
 And I'll bet that Mrs. Tinkle, as she looks from some direction
Is thinking, 'Maybe William really wrote with introspection.'"

William pushed upon the poem to smooth the lines away,
And Virginia said, "Let's frame it and share the thoughts today,
 For things are much too serious, and when we need a laugh,
You can read the first part, Bill, and I'll read the second half!"

THE SUBSTITUTE

"Hello! I'm Mrs. Madden, Sandwich Bay PTO,
I read you've volunteered your services if a teacher has to go
   Off to a special setting, or if by chance is sick,
Which is the case this morning and it's you by chance we pick.

"School's in session half a day, it's examination time,
And we need a proctor for Ms. Person's class, so often out of line.
   You'll just pass out papers and be assigned to oversee
A group of students nine of grade, but act the grade of three."

Virginia said, "I'm busy ... it seems the bees are back,
And William's cut some other wood for me to split and stack.
   But he is simply practicing piano here today,
So I'll send him off to take my place to watch the children play."

William said, "A piece of cake! I'll simply stand around,
And pencil on a paper what I see and hear profound."
   Thus William with his lunch box and a thermos full of juice,
Set off to tame the boys and girls — he'd not suffer their abuse!

The story he recorded in his normal rhyming fashion,
Is meant by him to entertain and not invite compassion.
   The story he recorded is by estimate quite true,
So read it friends — is proctoring a job you'd like to do?

Oh what a precious moment that I'm the chosen one,
To proctor this the class whose behavior's come undone.
   And monitor the progress that each boy and girl has made,
In a test of ninety minutes that will form the midyear grade.

Leo Carpenter

The yellow-sacked materials secured within the room,
And I as proctor at the front, my position here assume.
   Now call the children from the hall in manner calm and steady,
"Enter now, assume a seat and for testing let's be ready."

But they were having none of that and rolled around the floor,
Or shoved and jostled each about, now in and out the door.
   But who's in charge? — Me! William! — so I raised my voice and said,
"Come find a seat and settle in lest William here sees red!"

So, at the mention of my name each dropped into a seat,
To act in manner more grade nine, grown up and more discrete.
   And with pencils at the ready, each armed with number two,
There sat transfixed and waited for commands of what to do.

And I must say they did quite well,
As test and William wove the spell.
   A quiet place, a pin heard drop,
And each of mouth with lollipop.

While later at the PTO,
With special invite Bill would go,
   Awarded Tester of the Year,
Presented by — Virginia dear!

JUST OVERNIGHT

One hundred-twenty miles is the distance door to door,
If shorter were the distance the greetings would be more.
But once a month when weather's kind or other times between,
They'd feed the fish and pack the cats and join the travel scene.

Now Bill's not much for on the road but Virginia's taken by,
Birds and trees, fields and hills, anything she'll spy.
And depending on who's driving, the other gets the view,
Virginia's usually going, and Bill's when visit's through.

So over the bridge and down the roads that find the mountain's run,
To zigzag on the travel lanes to make the travel fun.
A turn into the quick foods place positioned on the way,
There freshen up and eat a muffin baked fresh yesterday.

Back upon the road they go, turn right to reach the gate,
Complain while paying toll for roads paid for since sixty-eight.
Now the ride's through towns and villages which point the daughter's place,
And finally the front door and the smile on daughter's face.

Now daughter is an outside girl who's always on the go,
Like a stick that travels in the stream, she's always in the flow.
She says, "Dad let's climb that mountain to see what mountains hide,
Or meet a person such as me coming up the other side.

"Let's walk down this embankment, how deep the river's cut,
Let's find some rocks and artifacts to find out which was what.
Let's trace the prints that made that path and animal pretend,
Then find another path and then another path again.

"Let's pick some herbs and spices and fruits which fill the tree,
For nature's goods are plentiful, are healthful and are free.
  Just stuff them in your pocket, Dad, when home we'll make a treat,
Of soup and breads and sweet things not at your home to eat."

  A day of conversation that carries to the night,
Daughter's time to tuck them in, saying, "Mom and Dad, sleep tight."
  They are richer for the visit and the novel things there seen,
While from their house to daughter's home and the places in between.

MOVING SOUTH

"Virginia, did you know our neighbor Ray across the way
Was wondering, on retirement, if Edna and he should stay
The whole year long in Sandwich Bay, or divide the time of year,
With six months north in the summertime and the rest go south of here?

"Seems his sister bought a place in a friendly southern clime,
Where sun shines through the last three months and first four all the time.
Where citrus fruits and avocados and tropical palm trees grow,
Where it's fifty steps across the sand to the Gulf of Mexico.

"Now doesn't that sound appealing to those the likes of us?
No more shoveling winter snow or other frigid fuss,
No more picky woolen scarfs that wrap from neck to arm,
No more heavy mittens to keep the fingers warm."

Virginia countered, "I've never seen the scarfs of which you talk,
And it's Tommy Todd the neighbors' boy who frees snow from the walk.
I'm here to keep the teapot and to play your favorite sound,
And we've the television to get warm and dance around.

"We have our church and social sets and friends to think about,
Will they even have a thought of us if we're gone, we're south, we're out?
And what of Kitty and Katrina? You know they hate the heat,
A new place would confuse them, what with sand spurs at their feet!"

William responded, "That's enough of that. I gather by your tone,
If it's south that I'll be moving, I'll be moving there alone.
And I know that what you're saying surely makes a lot sense,
But ... maybe we can visit if we ever have the chance."

Virginia said, "That's the man I married! A man who's never swayed,
A man who always thinks things out before he's on his way.
 I'm so proud of your decision to keep us where we're at,
Me, the scarf, the gloves, the friends, Katrina and Kitty Kat!"

DAY AFTER CHRISTMAS

'Twas the day after Christmas and William was seen,
Midst the cats and Virginia with presents between.
They had just settled down to go over the stack,
To see which gifts to keep and which things they'd bring back.

The cats in the ribbons and the seasonal wrap,
With one eye each open, spied the scene of attack.
For with so much to roll in and chase on the floor,
Time to jump for the ornaments, spring ever more.

William echoed the warning they had heard day and night,
"You cats to the kitchen, there to stay out of sight!
You've caused enough damage this seasonal time,
Trailing tinsel and bulbs in your Christmas tree climb."

Kitty and Katrina looked back as to say,
"What's got into our William that he's acting today,
As the Grinch whom we've heard in books often read,
In place of our ho-ho-ing Santa instead?"

William gave the eye back, then they bounded as one,
To sleep in a ball 'neath the dishes undone.

Virginia stood tall with a nightgown held high,
With the price on the tag indicating good buy.
But parrots and jungle life — wild for her taste,
Found the gown in the pile of the going back place.

At the same time was William in a shirt he'd received,
Trussed up in a size which Bill Jr. believed,
  Was the size of his father but was not the right one,
But rather the size of his father's grandson.
  Thus placed in the pile of sizes too small,
To be carried back later to the store in the Mall.

So on through the morning to the time after noon,
They shuffled through fashions they'd wear later or soon.
  Checked electric utensils, read instructions and then,
Placed high in the pantry — they'd not see them again.

From disorder came order, three piles in a row:
The stayers, the storers and the things which would go.
  And Bill said to Virginia, "It was a great day we had,
And this day after Christmas is itself not so bad."

Here the cats chose to enter, Kitty rubbed at Bill's feet,
While Katrina chose Ginny's lap as a seat.
  Now all four immersed in a soft season sound,
Which would cradle the old year and bring new year 'round.

SKATING

"Virginia ... I see there's a special at the Mall's Figure Eights,
Toboggans, sleds and puffy coats, skis and poles and skates.
  The last is to me of interest, and though years and years are by,
I think I'll purchase hockey types and give the ice a try."

  Virginia responded, "Don't be foolish Bill, remember brittle bone,
But if you decide the ice to try, the try'll be not alone.
  Do they maybe make a mention of some figure skates for girls?
For if they do, I'll pick a pair to try figure eights and twirls.
  And maybe all the fancy moves, the jumps and spins and such,
Could return in little time, I may yet have the touch."

  William now beside her said, "Don't tell me I've a champ,
Who sits with me on winter eves and shares the reading lamp?"
  She said, "The proof will be the pudding and the pudding will be nice,
When you lace the skates upon the lass and lead her to the ice!"

  Both were most excited as they entered Figure Eights,
Intent upon procuring hockey blades and figure skates.
  And the clerk was most congenial, "May I help you elders out?"
With Bill's response, "The skate department's what it's all about."

  The clerk then stretched his arms and said, "They're gone, the adult buys,
The only skates now left for ice are of the children's size.
  But the two of you are lucky, for with the same amount to spend,
If you'll change your call for winter fun and try tobogganing."

  Bill's eyes sparkled at Virginia and Virginia gazed at Bill,
And he said, "The rink is quite a walk away, but backyard starts a hill.
  So why not a four-seater to wrap and take away?
Then night or day, with cats aboard, we'll coast to Sandwich Bay!"

The moonlight saw them halfway down on a path between the trees,
With Virginia in the forward station resting back against Bill's knees.
   Bill at rear the navigator, and you know behind him sat,
With flagging scarfs and tasseled hats — Katrina and Kitty Kat!

THE REFRIGERATOR

"Virginia, come and hear the sound the refrigerator makes,
Something starts to coming on, but it stops and then it shakes,
And then it starts to whining and then it starts to click,
Something in it tells me our preserver has gone sick."

Virginia said to check the wire to be sure the plug is in,
And maybe shake the ice box to make the spinner spin.
But I said, "Dear it's more than that, I think it's given out,
So let's take a ride and get a paper, check the sales we hear about.

"Since the day is Sunday and there're no deliveries today,
We'll put the food out in a box, let winter have its way.
Then take apart the reefer and place it in the shed,
And have it hold my many tools which rest on the floor instead.

"So we've lost the old refrigerator — nothing lasts forever,
Be thankful that it's wintertime and the food's kept by the weather.
Let's think back upon the pilgrims with no electric plugs,
To energize their pantry and store their food and jugs.

"Let's think about Columbus and the men who sailed the seas,
Who only tasted salted food, no meat or frozen peas.
Let's think about the desert travelers, only fruit and camel's milk,
Let's think about the gypsies and their goods in bags of silk ..."

Virginia said, "Please stop it, Bill, you're taking it too far!
Everything you mention goes back from where we are.
And while you've rambled on and on there's a bargain that I found,
In the section of the *Church News* titled *Second Time Around*.

"It seems a couple's off to somewhere and they're selling all they've got,
The kitchen stove, the washer, a twelve-quart cooking pot.
  But the fact that brought attention stated, *'Get it while it's cold,
The perfect size to fit your kitchen and it's only two years old.'*"

FLYING SOUTH

William standing, shivering, snow well above his knees,
The wind a chariot for season's snow through leafless winter trees.
Picky woolen scarf wrapped tight upon the ear,
And chatter from now clicking teeth alone the listeners hear.

Cats stare through frosted window, their purrs in tone convey,
"Better here upon the sill than the other side today!"

William wished away a foot of snow as he stepped down to the drive,
Now up the stairs and through the door where warmer souls abide.
Through winter's breath called, "Dear Virginia, I've something on my mind
Which I feel that I must introduce this biting winter time.

"Recall the invitation which the Wiggins tendered us,
The day I spoke of sunny south and no more frigid fuss?
Well, my toes are mostly frozen and ... if it's all the same with you,
Your William craves an ocean time with sun and skies of blue."

Virginia shouted, "Happy birthday! Though it's still two weeks away,
I read your mind a month ago and packed you yesterday.
Tomorrow at eleven your plane departs the gate,
And the Wiggins and puppies on the gulf sands there await."

So William now a flyer was high above the land,
He off to splash the water, to build castles in the sand,
Collect each shell he fancies, and walk the wave-drawn line,
To feel the sun that changes moods from cold to summer time.

And indeed the time was merry as his blood began to thin,
And the spring was back into his step, but his mind was wandering.
He thought about Virginia where in iciness she sat,
He thought about Katrina, and also Kitty Kat.

Two days and something stirring in the Wiggins' southern home,
For Bill returning from a walk, thinking he was there alone,
   Found his heart begin to pounding with the sign pinned to the wall,
HAPPY BIRTHDAY WILLIAM! HAPPY BIRTHDAY FROM US ALL!

Well my friends, I'm sure you've guessed it, for that's Virginia's way,
That she, just two days after Bill, had come to join the play,
   Along with Kitty and Katrina on their little kitties' leash,
There to walk along, a quartet, on the gulf shore's sunny beach!

SPANISH MACKEREL

   Aboard the vessel *Perigee*, of the salty fishing kind,
William hooked twelve mackerel on a line he trolled behind.
   He'd share his oily trophies at Saturday's covered dish,
Where friends would bring surprises to complement caught fish....

   He hovered o'er the barbecue that fouled the bay side air,
Where flying birds with smarting eyes lay legless over there.
   Covered dishes bubbled midst southern ladies' glee,
And men were flush with winter's sun which dropped quickly to the sea.

   The coals had gone from red to black and William, most concerned,
For Spanish mackerel smoked uncooked from charcoal damp unburned.
   Here Virginia stepped outside the door as the deeds inside were done,
"Just how much longer, Darling? The women's wine's near gone!"

   He frowned atop his glasses as Virginia stepped inside,
Then checked the mackerel — still not done — a threat to cooker's pride!
   His brow began to sweating for the stove would not respond,
And stomachs heard were growling for fish to chew upon.

   Well ... the final call was offered, "Everybody take your place!"
Where Bill would offer sushi finely carved to fill the face.
   But front door's bell did save the day as the man from Fisherman's Shack
Said, "Fried fish for Bill from the *Perigee*, well-done with outer-skin black!"

ARTHUR'S TREASURE

   William on his bicycle along that stretch of road,
Which showed the dunes of whitened sands millenniums bestowed,
   Was put off from his purpose — a ride and then a swim,
By a vendor's tag of interest in a yard across from him.

        A PUFFY WHITE SLEEP SOFA
        WITH STITCHED-IN LINES OF BLUE,
        FOR THOSE WHO'LL COME TO VISIT
        WHO WILL SPEND A DAY OR TWO.
        THE MATTRESS, WHILE IT'S TOLERABLE
        HAS SEEN A BETTER DAY,
        AND YOUR COMPANY, WITH ACHING BACKS,
        WILL UP AND ON THEIR WAY.

   William squeezed the handle and performed a right oblique,
And rode a rocky terrace for a moment there to speak,
   To the matronly dispenser of the goods there strewn about,
Who called shrilly, "Husband Arthur, there are patrons, please come out!"
   But Arthur couldn't hear her for he frolicked in the surf,
Where he looked out towards the dolphins and what dolphins there observe

   "It's the sofa sleeper sign which screeched my wheels to stop,"
William offered to the madam within umbrella's shaded spot.
   The woman called attention to the absence of her spouse,
Saying, "I must tend this station, it seems Arthur's left the house."

   Now William joined with others, intrigued by seller's sign,
And weaved about the tables in a figure-eightish line,
   And engaged in conversation, which seemed appropriate of place,
And heard the lady hawking glass and cracking crystal plates.

Here William moved a basket and saw an object which it blocked,
A rustic pot with bell upon from old-time ticking clock,
  Quite unlike anything he had ever seen before,
Heard, "Arthur's treasure boils an egg and sometimes boils much more.
  For the pressure in the vessel, when the boiling point is reached,
Sends a spray of pushing water and the timing bell's released."

So the man who'd sought the sofa where visitors might rest,
Intrigued by Arthur's treasure bought the pot and headed west,
  To that spot so frequently chosen where he'd frolic in the surf,
And like Arthur, view the dolphins and what dolphins there observe.

MATILDA MORRISEY — SLIP COVERS

   The brochure slipped beneath the door signed, Matilda Morrisey,
Emblazoned there a picture of a chair of history.
   It spoke of chair disguises when one's seen better day,
And appearance states the option, the chair be cast away.
   Appended commendations affixed for significant work she'd done,
One was most impressive — a Presidential one:

*"Matilda made the slips where the king and queen once sat,
Which secreted the scratch marks of Chelsea's favorite cat."*

   William said, "An impressive communication Virginia, don't you think?
And a timely opportunity for black leather over pink.
   For you see I feel quite silly when Ray Wiggins comes to call,
And I'm sitting midst the roses and the pinkness of it all."

   "Then have Matilda over, Bill, to show the sample lot,
And maybe other compliments along the way she got."
   "You call! It's more a woman's thing, this fabric on a chair,
As for me ... I'm in the garden shed, as a bird house needs repair."

   So Virginia on the telephone ... and Matilda on the road,
Then through the front door shortly with materials she showed.
   Well, they talked about the leather, Matilda said, "That's not for you!
You are more a type for silkiness, with background baby-blue."
   And pointing to the picture of the product on display,
Said, "Virginia, you must have them, there can be no other way!

   "You are very fortunate, as I have those slips with me,
I'll run outside to fetch them. Might you fetch a pot of tea?"
   The tea now set for steeping, the slips set on the chair,
And Matilda and Virginia sipped in conversation there.

Leo Carpenter

William through the back door now, a birdhouse in his hand,
Thinking, "Me upon the leather will be masculine and grand!"
But here he entered on the ladies in their partnership of blue,
The chair in which he, William, sits and of Virginia's too.

Matilda said, "William, what a bird house, how talented you are!
I'll bet the birds are lining up from near and from afar.
And if birds would be a buyer they'd purchase theirs from you,
Your dimensions are proportional, the perfect home for two!"

Thus William's tongue now twisted said, "Matilda, could you spare
Some little scraps of leather for some coasters here and there?
For leather looks so manly when it's set beside the blue,
And will give our cups a resting place as we share our tea for two."

GUEST SPEAKER

William hugged Virginia, then a peck upon the cheek,
Facts packed within the briefcase he relied upon to speak,
   William stepped beyond the doorway and there set his briefcase down,
To flush the twirlies from the hood of the Town Car which they'd found.

   The green within the rivulets trailed to the tar below,
As William cranked the engine, now off to speak he'd go.
   Thirty miles the highway as speakers sang their song,
William tapped the steering wheel and if familiar, sang along.

   An hour's time the travel, now find the city hall,
SPECIAL GUEST — WILLIAM ALTONBERRY, there posted on the wall.
   It was then the fact would surface, his pressure rose then fell,
An emptiness of stomach noting William was not well.

   For within that very instant the realization came,
His bag of information and address home were both the same.
   Now the hall door swung to open and the audience arose,
"My friends, here's William Altonberry, to report the things he knows."

   Yet just one fact was evident to William at the time,
His bag of knowledge sat alone beneath a front yard pine.
   His hands arose, the palms expressed the wish for all to sit,
As William digging deeply searched for Altonberry wit.

   Then a messenger walked a center stage, presenting William with this note:
I found your case a riverboat, midst twirlies and afloat.
   And I know how much you need it when you wish to speak your best,
So, at ten o'clock the bag arrives via Federal Express.

Now William gazed down at his watch which read nine fifty-nine,
In just another minute the thoughts within the bag are mine.
Then at that very instant heard, "Is there an Altonberry here?"
And came the bag with message — *Knock 'em dead, my William dear!*

THE RAFFLE

   The Altonberry's backyard birch filtered May Day's noontime sun,
Projecting leaf-like shadows on the billowed clouds above.
   Today's weather most inviting so that indoors chases out,
Here William and Virginia and the kitties spring about.

   "Is anybody out there?" came the call beyond the gate,
Then Virginia's cheery, "Over here, beside the picnic plate."
   And in an instant stood beside them the Girl Scouts Cookies pair,
Who held up raffle tickets and fanned them in the air.

   Now with a practiced perfect overture Anita sang the plea,
"Would you buy a chance to see the game from Mary Ann and me?"
   William questioned kindly, "What are the chances for?"
The girl's retort was, "Major League, with the proceeds for the poor."

   William's smile acknowledged then, a ticket sale's assured,
He said "One each for Virginia and the cats and mine makes four."
   Here the cats beneath the table with the mention of their name,
Slapped around the yarn ball — they'd be ready for the game!

   Currency for chance exchanged, the girls skipped through the gate,
And shouted back, "The drawing's the ninth when the hour reaches eight.
   We'll call if there's a winner, and we're wishing you success,
For everything that's asked of you results with nods and yes!"

   On the evening designated at quarter past the hour,
With William into *Wall Street* and Virginia's elbows flour,
   The ringing phone uncradled and while William's words were none,
He heard the jubilation, "You won! You won! You won!

"There are tickets for the ball game plus a fancy dinner fare,
And a special bonus limousine to take you here and there.
  And ... you may choose two special friends to bring along to see,
What makes the local boys of summer springtime's cup of tea."

Well, the details of the special day are many to recount —
The ride, the food and conversation as the crowd would wave and shout.
  And those who watched on television, down the third base line was seen,
The raffle-winning Altonberrys and two friends in Girl Scout green!

SUMMER COTTAGE

  An electrifying situation was confronted by the pair,
For as Virginia closed the window a spark repelled her hair,
  And her feet were set to dancing as she grounded to the floor,
And she called about for William with his broom outside the door.

  "Come here, Darling, and touch this very spot,
To see if what's electrical mirrors that which I just got!"
  William said, "You're overacting Dear, maybe static is to blame,"
But when he touched "this very spot," his jolt — the very same!

  William said, "I warned you Dear, the Wiggins they were right,
The water tastes as iodine and the mattress — bugs' delight.
  The dirt road leaves no traction and my wheels just spin around,
While the midnight boaters' motors make for sleeping less than sound.
  And I'd bet the juice the window gets is ample and enough,
To harness the refrigerator that melts our frozen stuff.

  "Sure, the manager was congenial when the money was exchanged,
When he said the place was shipshape with just a few things to arrange,
  Such as haze which coats the windows and the tracks upon the rugs,
And the holes which ride the summer screens like swinging doors for bugs.

  "And they said if we had problems that they would be around,
But all my effort simply proves that no one's to be found.
  For I've tried to reach the office, but the help is out of town —
Probably enjoying a vacation at some other camping ground!"

Leo Carpenter

SAILING SAILING

You might deem it improbable those of Altonberry age
Would be taken by a westerly, they'd add a nautical page.
   Nonetheless it's factual, the nature of the pair,
Thus FOR SALE from yacht's aft rail, a sign a ship's to share.

   Just a week before Regatta, shipshape work to do,
Shine the bell and polish chrome, sailor's work for two.
   Kitty and Katrina, he at aft and she at fore,
Each one eye upon the master, the other sea to shore.
   The cats aboard heard salty words the hands would cast about,
Rope was line, port and starboard, green go, red right out.

   A place to sleep's a cabin, swab the floor's a deck,
Draw in on the luffing sail, Castle Point's a wreck.
   Tides and currents high and swift, beacons' bells at sea,
Navigational and nautical ... now, cat nap sets cats free.

   A week to master in and out as the crew rolled up and down,
And the sail was lofted high each day from the rings the mast around,
   Where sheet would seek the weather vane which wind pushed side to side,
As the four aboard would weave the waves and study books of tide.

   The shakedown cruise now underway, the sail was full and drawn,
Salty cats from cushions through portholes watched land gone.
   Here William used the muscle, while of course, Virginia's sailed before,
And she surely called the orders as the sea replaced the shore.

   And they headed up to tack a line, a zigzag of direction,
And William heard the captain and took sailing education.
   She said, "It's similar to the Town Car, Bill, with the wind replacing gas,
Where the speed is secondary and the charts will point our path.

The Altonberrys of Sandwich Bay

Just keep an eye upon the compass, check the tide and pilot plan,
Sight the point which we are leaving and the point upon we'll land."

So out and back and in and out, for days the sailors sailed,
And took their turn at coursing wheel or cushions at the rail.
  And the Sandwich Bay Regatta showed *Recess* in the lead,
On a day of eighteen knots the wind — a perfect Altonberry breeze!

The command was, "William, you be master and I will be the mate,
We'll race the others from the mark, then return the starting gate."
  So William wore the captain's cap, with Virginia there the hand,
And the cats showed proud their telltale tails away and back to land.

So *Recess* chased the markers and the cannon called the race,
And the ribbons were awarded and the blue one read, 1ST PLACE!
  Then the four stood on the platform and were called upon to say,
How novice captain ran the course and won Regatta Racing Day.

When asked, "How such accomplishment?" he cast his love a glance,
And the cats were staring questioningly as were racers from the stands.
  William took the microphone, and not rehearsed or planned,
Said, "I merely brought her in and out as I sailed from the seat of my pants."

Virginia thought, "That's William," as the cats each winked an eye,
"He prefers to be a layman, for no matter how I try,
  To acclimate him to the manuals of technical expertise,
His 'seat of pants' philosophy seems to place his mind at ease."

Well, friends, no matter how accomplished, the ribbon hangs in frame —
William Altonberry and crew won the regatta racing game!

THE WISHING STONE

William found a wishing stone
As he walked the beach about,
 Round and gray — the skipper sort —
A thumb's print centered out.

He whispered, "The wonder of a wishing stone,
Just rub the thumb-worn spot,
 And ponder what you've little of,
And fancy that you've not."

Here William rubbing, contemplating,
Was concerned when asking for,
 The simplest little pleasure,
When those with less need more.

Thus turned and faced the ocean,
Whose waves had brought the stone,
 Tossed and watched it skip away,
Five times ... then sink alone.

And as the skipper skimmed away,
William wished the phrase,
 "May the finder next be blessed as I,
In a multitude of ways!"

PITSY AND PENNY

Pitsy and Penny were out through the hole,
Which they'd dug 'neath the fence near the flag-holding pole.
The work had been tedious but the feeling was great,
As they entered Bill's yard through the open side gate.

The cry for the puppies filled the neighborhood air,
For the Wiggins were searching high — low — everywhere!
"Here Pitsy! Here Penny! Come to Mommy and Dad!"
But the dogs were elusive, were hard to be had.
They were out for the hunt with their thinking, canine,
To chase Kitty and Katrina at the top of their mind.

But the cats were conscious of the dogs' goings on,
As they slapped at fish in the yard's goldfish pond.
They winked at each other in felinish play,
And sat there conspicuous, meowing away.

Bill had heard some commotion in the moonlighted night,
Cause to step to the porch with Virginia at right.
A flick of the switch and the yard came to day,
And the dogs saw the cats, and the cats thought — "Away!"

Pitsy the poodle made a dash down the path,
He leaped 'cross the pond, but only made half!
The look on his face was startled and grim,
He had come for the cats, not for fish or a swim!

Hot on his heels, Penny averted the pond,
But went fast to the briars with the prickers upon.
She yelped in displeasure, then a bolt for the street,
Where she waited the wet one, to plan their retreat.

LEO CARPENTER

Approaching the yard now were Edna and Ray,
With flashlights and leashes to harness their prey.
  The hunted were grateful and jumped in the air,
Thought, "Enough of this action, take us home, take us there!"

  Kitty Kat and Katrina weaved a cat's figure-eight,
Through the legs of Virginia and Bill by the gate,
  While the Wiggins did collar their Pitsy and Pen,
And scolded, "No holes, you two — ever again!"

DR. KUREM

William waited nervously in the patient's plastic chair,
Nurse Feeney, mustering up a smile, asked the reason he was there.
   William wailed, "My nose is stuffed and my joints feel aging pain,
Plus a myriad of other things in the anatomical domain!"

   "You know the process Mr. Altonberry, Dr. Kurem's on his way
From Mrs. Johnson's Billy, who scraped his knee at play.
   So, disrobe and please be ready for the doctor's precious time,
And practice what you'll say to him, you're next in doctor's line."

   William in his johnny — his favorite color blue —
Reluctantly climbed the table of the doctor's point of view.
   And his teeth began to chatter as cold now gripped his knees,
And he looked about for tissue to restrain projected sneeze.

   He gazed about the cubicle and strained an idle ear,
Listened to the goings on of medics working near.
   Heard some grunts and groaning from neighbors being probed,
Heard other checking chatter from those supposed disrobed.

   William carried to the cabinet which held the doctor's stock,
The sticks and swabs and ointments and the forms for doctor's talk.
   And his palms began to sweating as he practiced what he'd say,
Here the doctor stepped into the room with, "How are you today?"

   William's knees began to warming and his toes began to twist,
His body filled with surging blood, he forgot his ailment list,
   Told the doctor, "I feel fine! I've curtailed my appetite,
I exercise each morning and sleep long throughout the night."

The doctor monitored his pressure, found his sugar hadn't soured,
Said, "Mr. Altonberry, I've concluded you're physically empowered.
   Just keep up what you're doing and write a note to me,
And I'll pass it on to others who aspire to seventy-three.

   "If you think of something else not covered here today,
You can call me at the country club where all the doctors play.
   I would continue eating all that Virginia cooks for you,
And remind her that her time with me is three months overdue."

   William whistled as he exited the heavy metal door,
And waved to whimpering children dropping blocks upon the floor.
   Happy his condition, as far as the monitors portray,
Should keep him up and running for at least this present day!

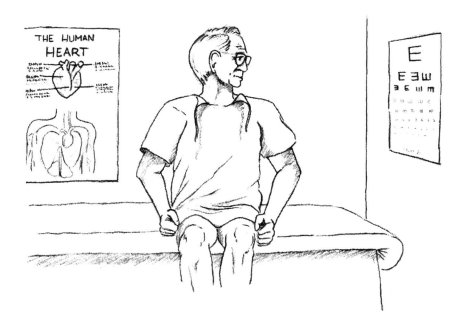

HANDY'S HARDWARE STATION

William was complaining, he had other things in mind,
Than to sit outside the sewing store and waste warm morning's time,
For spring coursed through his vessels and his muscles pulsed away,
A shovel in the garden seemed more appropriate today.

Gin had said, "I'm just a minute for some buttons and some bows,
As a summer dress lacks both of these to return to wearing clothes.
And I'm sure that when you see me in the product I envision,
You'll agree that just one moment's time was not an imposition."

William spun his cap about and watched her as she went,
And thought, Virginia is quite frugal for with minor money spent,
She'll have a fancy dress for our Sunday morning ride,
When my fancy fashion model, in vogue sits by my side.

But what's to do while waiting as Virginia shops around?
Perhaps a tool from Handy's Hardware and free coffee's to be found.
Maybe garden conversation where the cultivators hang,
Or peruse the aisle of cutting tools and metal things that bang.

"Hello there, Bill!" said Handy, "it's great to see you friend,
And inform you you're the millionth man to push the front door in!"
As he handed him the cloak and crown which befit the celebration,
Of the millionth man to step inside Handy's Hardware Station.

Oom-pah-pahs of Dixieland while cameras cranked away,
Balloons rose to the ceiling and confetti fell his way,
While the Mayor of Sandwich Bay — with politics in mind —
Pushed a shopper's cart of flowers down the celebration line.

William was quite taken and was sweating with surprise,
As well-wishers pushed to greet him, some with envy of the eyes,
  For had they known the number they'd have squeezed inside before
William Altonberry pushed the millionth swinging door.

  William left encumbered with a multitude of things,
Tools and plaques and coupons that winning often brings.
  And he placed them on the front seat for Virginia to see,
Then waited as she exited Monique's Boutiquery.

  Virginia leaned upon the car while William carried on,
About his timed good fortune and his many prizes won.
  She smiled and then reminded him good fortune came his way,
Through her need for bows and buttons on this millionth person day!

THE BULKHEAD DOOR

    As William looked out from his cellar, through bulkhead door was seen,
A thousand points of midday light with a thousand there between.
    For the paint in layers, dried and cracked, had little left to give,
Thus precipitation dripped on through as water drips the sieve.

    "What must I do to solve this?" A dilemma William faced,
Contemplating reconstruction, his builder's mind a'race.
    "Should I overlay with plastic or fiberglass the door,
Or let coffee tins collect the drops which river up the floor?

    "I think I'll go replacement as Wiggins last year had done,
In fact, procurement's galvanized — I'll get the rustproofed one!
    But first the project which I face is to have the old door gone,
So I'll go and fetch the proper tools to bang and cut upon."

    The minds of backyard tinkerers, and the sounds the tinkerers make,
Found William flanked by experts soon, with suggestions wise to take.
    Ray Wiggins viewed the waterfall and offered, "Rust has fixed the screws,
Thus a cutting torch and chisel here seem necessary news."

    Other technical terms as pressure treated, crowbar and a sledge,
Block and tackle, come-along, inclined plane's a wedge,
    Wheel and axle, elbow grease, on and on the flow,
With the only fact agreed upon — the bulkhead door must go!

    Above renovation conversation, the garden gate's heard squeak,
Tommy Todd, with stage the sawhorse, having listened, here would speak.
    "Your grownup thoughts are complicated, let me offer this suggestion,
A children's slide atop each door for H_2O deflection.
    And my plan serves double purpose for both rain and youngsters' play,
For Mr. Altonberry's rainy cellar, and for children's sunny day."

Well, laughter filled the afternoon as the experts eyed the boy,
"A bulkhead's architectural, the slide's a children's toy!"
  But William interceded here on the side of youth,
For in the rafters of the gardener's shed lay the **very slides** he'd use.

  And indeed the reconstruction was done that very day,
And seven neighbors' children and the cats did slide away.
  And further purpose of the placement came with the evening's rain,
For the water rode the bulkhead's slide to the street ... then down the drain!

THE ALTONBERRYS OF SANDWICH BAY

SANDWICH BAY PARADE

    For this Independence Day occasion marching bands here congregated,
And clustered balloons, lighter than air, lifted vendor's hand and waited.
    And children tugged at mothers' skirts pleading pennants passing by,
While lady fingers smoked and popped on this Fourth Day of July.

    Red fire engine's siren sang atop the clang of bells,
And the cotton candy carriage man cries other sweets he sells.
    And policemen riding iron horses caution children back,
And the mayor and the councilmen walk the covered trolley track.

    The Boy Scouts and their master hear the drums that fill the air,
And the line of march is crooked as they turn to see who's there.
    And this one hops one-footed as his heel's been marched upon —
Perhaps intentionally by that one who smirks and skips along!

    The Girl Scouts — practice perfect — are ready for the time,
For right is right and left is left and flawless is their line.
    "Oh beautiful for spacious skies," sing patriotic song,
Their heels heard *click* and skirts heard *swish* so smartly step along!

    The floats are some in number dressed red and white and blue,
And children stand upon them and wave a flag or two.
    And the dog who'd jumped the picket fence's barking fills the air,
As sopranos wearing powdered wigs spitting high notes disappear.

    The brass which blasted *oom-pah-pahs* and the trombones' sliding fare,
The trumpets and the clashing cymbals stopped just over there.
    And the drummers tap their *rat-tat-tat*, the bass a measured *boom*,
And smartly step past where I stand to John Sousa's music tune!

To my surprise there's William, with Virginia at his side,
A banner on the Duesenberg — CO-MARSHALS SIT INSIDE!
  For of all the dignitaries prominent hereabout,
He and she the couple chosen, for whom observers shout!

  It was hardly half an hour when the final dimming drum,
Turned smart into the common where the speaking would be done.
  And the men who seek election would puff out from the stage,
To introduce the patriots who had written history's page.

  The children would turn cartwheels and balloons would trail a string,
And committee men in huddle for next year's figuring,
  For there would be another where the patriotic played,
Where the flags wave to the music of the Sandwich Bay Parade!

WHEEL WOBBLE

While fast upon the cycle trail on a day seemed heaven sent,
William sensed a wobble, Virginia said, "A wheel seems bent."
William said, "It's hard to move ahead when the motion's side to side,"
As he searched his bag for remedy to continue on the ride.

The cycle now inverted, the wheels addressed the sky,
And William motioned others to stay left when passing by.
The tool case from the seat was freed and William searched to find,
The proper tool for wobbled wheels to come back into line.

But nonesuch was apparent and William seemed concerned,
That the pedaling was over and to home they must return,
When Virginia gave directions for her front fork to his rear,
And to place the chain for movement upon his pedaling gear.

So William took instruction and their transportation grew,
From bicycles for each of them, to a bicycle built of two!
William said, "You're marvelous!" but Virginia's quick reply,
"Let's pedal fast and pedal past those who snickered passing by!"

THE HOUSE OF THE SEVEN GABLES

There was momentary confusion within the car that day,
For The House of the Seven Gables was historically miles away.
But sure enough within ten miles of where the Altonberrys reside,
Sat a distinctive house which filled one block plus half a block besides.

A common sign of address was affixed to the proper house,
Which stated, SEVEN GABLES WITHIN PLUS THE SEVEN GABLES' SPOUSE.
Each pair bequeathed a gable which was added to the sum,
To accommodate each couple with the two — now married — one.
Thus the Gable's homes were contiguous, beginning with the main,
For mature and married Gables would adjoin their house to same.

Now the Altonberrys and others from about and Sandwich Bay,
Pay a dollar for admission there to wile an hour away
In the house of the Seven Gables — not the famed of Salem, Mass. —
But the house ten miles from Sandwich Bay, which curious travelers pass.

The Altonberrys of Sandwich Bay

THE AFTER PARTY

   The bells which rang out earlier were a sign of things to be,
For the steepled church across the town kept wedding company,
   Where was seen a trail of limousines and the tails of men in black,
There preceded through the churchyard by eight maids with open back.
   Here attitudes seemed somber, not as something would be gained,
And greetings seemed too casual and handshakes some restrained.

   Some were young and some were old, some with canes to give support,
There were ties and buttoned collars, summer coats of formal sort.
   For middle morning nuptials would bond acquainted pair,
And the bells did ring and coats were off and confetti filled the air.
   And the congregation exited to organ's playing sound,
And sopranos strained to reach the notes and limos loped around.

   Beside the curb a lacy card obscure to observation,
The Gothic print showed time and place and seating reservation.
   And also noted further, celebration would abide,
At a home just half a block from where the Altonberrys reside.
   There in stately Dutch colonial where the Hooligans now live,
The parents of the groom will the after party give.

   When Bill arrived at home with the bread and paper sought,
He mentioned of the wedding seen while getting what he got.
   And Virginia said, "I knew of that for the Hooligans had sent
A neighborly invitation, with our attendance their intent."
   So William waited casual, clothed contemporary style,
And sat and scanned his paper and though anxious read a while.

   Some time before the day was down leaden skies appeared,
And the caterer's finger sandwiches and pastries it was feared,
   Would be soddened by a downpour on the elegant affair,
And guests sought sheltering overhangs or umbrellas over chair.

However, rain was of the bucket type, and dancing had begun,
Imbibers shared the microphone and drinking songs were sung.
　And the bellies filled with plenty and acquaintances were made,
And the ushers hugged the maidens as the maidens smoked away.

　And Bill played his harmonica and Virginia played her song,
And the youngsters and the oldsters and the infants sang along.
　And newlyweds set travel to resorts away from here,
Amid the cries, "Best wishes!" "Long life!" "Forever cheer!"

THE FRONT WINDOW

   Do you recall the time Virginia put William on a plane,
To visit with the Wiggins in their southerly domain?
   Although his time to visit would conclude in just a week,
Her surprise to him would be the cats and she would seek
   The man sent on vacation to free him from the snow,
And they would join their William, walk along where he would go.

   Well ... Raymond's house, their residence, the time that they were there,
Was in daytime filled with sunshine but in darkness night's chilled air.
   And William who was longing for a thing to bang upon,
Weighed that present drafty windows if replaced would keep nights warm.
   The man sent on vacation to free him from the snow,
Thought about some three weeks' work with four days but to go.

   Quick, a window felt his hammer and the pitted metal bent,
But Virginia as well as Edna and the cats now less content,
   Were quick to find an open door and with picnic basket packed,
Said, "William, we've some things to see, we'll see you when we're back."
   The man sent on vacation to free him from the snow,
Waved off then to the party steering south past beach house row.

   William, through the window's hole, now more aware of pounding surf,
Looked out upon some faces there collected to observe.
   Each of these an "expert" from the Handy Person's School,
With most prominent among them, the master Dick O'Tool.
   The man sent on vacation to free him from the snow,
Was gawked upon through gaping hole, the stage for builder's show.

Leo Carpenter

The crowd now up to face him, they without while he within,
Were bubbling with suggestions where improvements should begin.
   But William called attention that his tools rest back at home,
When Dick O'Tool, the master said, "Fear not, I've lots to loan."
   The man sent on vacation to free him from the snow,
Watched the front wall and the side walls and the back wall as they'd go.

   Virginia along with Edna and the cats at destination,
Thought back about the project and the man upon vacation,
   And wondered at day's end, would some rubble still be there?
Would the front room and the others feel the open outside air?
   The man sent on vacation to free him from the snow,
Was looked upon with question by those who love him so.

   The sketches on the kitchen table, crude and quickly drawn,
Showed open studs and wires clipped and pipes once there were gone.
   And the gazers all were workers and they worked to Dick's command —
You remember Dick, the master, who had every tool at hand?
   The man sent on vacation to free him from the snow,
Watched the workers and the windows and the walls once there now go.

   The telephone incessant, and deliveries were made,
The gawkers now were builders and their bodies made parade.
   And the spaces once there vacant were filled and shiny new,
With glass replacing fallen brick and wind replaced by view.
   The man sent on vacation to free him from the snow,
Was sizzling with excitement as he watched a new house grow!

   The caterer had just arrived, the tables now were spread,
For Dick O'Tool and he himself and others must be fed.
   For they had set a record and had shown what can be done,
When a man has all the tools you need and workers work as one.
   The man sent on vacation to free him from the snow,
Would take a name and address as new friends waved to go.

Twilight was the picture and the sun had left the sky,
While William waited anxiously, but watched as they drove by.
  A thought there fell upon him, "They did not recognize
The newness of the structure and have casually passed the drive!"
  The man sent on vacation to free him from the snow,
Waved a greeting from the highway — it was William whom they know!

  Virginia was astounded, Edna Wiggins shed a tear,
The left side was the right side and the front was now the rear.
  And the cats filled with confusion had to learn another way,
For the front door was the back door to the yard where kitties play.
  The man sent on vacation to free him from the snow,
Helped build the place that Dick had drawn with just four days to go!

PAPEETE, TAHITI

In the travel agent's office where windows were adorned,
With cardboard women in bikinis in intriguing places, warm,
  Holding drinks with pink umbrellas with expressions, "Here's to you!"
Waited William and Virginia with a brochure each to view.

  The ad within the paper they had seen that very day,
Said, *Come to see the places where the Polynesians play!*
  And Virginia with her travel prize from the Bayside Flower Show,
Offered thereupon to William, "That's the place for us to go!
  For you know my love of flowers and Tahiti's prominent
For bougainvillea, frangipani, as well as others you have sent."

  William checked Alaska for a flight soon off to Nome,
But was reminded by Virginia of the wintertime at home,
  And the winds which wail across the bay and plague him every year,
And William said, "Tahiti sounds just fine, Virginia dear.
  For Nome shows icy mountains as the ocean rolls and heaves,
Maybe better under coconut trees and walled pandanus leaves."

  Kiran came to greet them for they were next in line,
He thanked them for their patronage of Kiran's Travel Time.
  As he clicked on his computer and the numbers filled the screen,
He pointed to the places which friends and he had seen.
  Then Virginia waved Tahiti (in William's pocket, Nome),
A tropical destination would be theirs away from home.

Alas! came disappointment in the flashing WAITING LIST,
"But there's another way to get there, if on Tahiti you insist,
For there's a line called Air Alaska with a vacancy for two,
That's off for Nome tomorrow that I can book for you.
The words that sit before me show adjoining vacant seats,
On Wednesday to Polynesia and the port town of Papeete."

William thought, "What a coincidence, he must have read my mind,
We'll get to see Alaska and Tahiti both this time!
Virginia gets her flowers while mine a flier's view,
Of Nome within Alaska, plus a French possession too!"

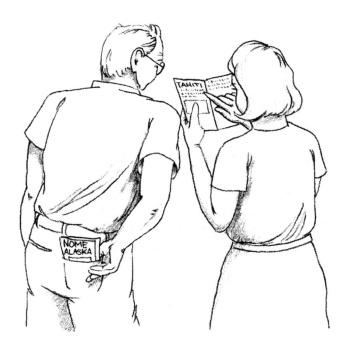

Leo Carpenter

THE SONG

Have you ever given second thoughts to the tune in William's head,
Wondered of the piano which sang out the tune instead?
Have you thought about Virginia's words, did they complement the tune,
On occasion think romantic in the summertime in June?

Well ... one early morn while passing, I heard their harmony,
Above the snare and snap of sticks, a drum surprise to me.
For I couldn't recall that instrument within the music group,
Of the ukulele, harmonica or the piccolo he'd toot.

Was there someone come to visit? In my curiosity,
I up'd the stairs and rapped the door to see who might it be.
As usual, the four of them — don't forget the cats —
Arrived to greet the rapper having left their sharps and flats.

Bill asked, "What are you selling, Tom?" For that's the way he spoke,
Never just "Hello! Come in!" but the ever present joke.
And I'm not one to drag my heels, responding, "I'm here to see
What brought an end to neighbor's sleep — the song of mystery."

Here, Bill stepped back and Kitty's tail in plain sight there to see,
Was stepped upon by master and the cat sang out in G!
Bill exclaimed, "I'm sorry!" Possibly Kitty's thinking too —
To lie beneath elevens, the size within your shoe!

However, cats' tails are resilient, though some crooked from the crunch,
But off to crouch behind the couch, the tail will heal's the hunch.
Katrina, arched against the wall, chose to follow now we three,
To the music room where sounds abound and to keep house homely.

The Altonberrys of Sandwich Bay

At just about this point in time came Virginia's repartee,
"Come along and listen, Thomas, but listen secretly.
For we're just about middle of the part I call refrain,
The bridge is built with words now written, mysterious yet plain.

"Am I correct in my assumption it's the early morning sound,
Of Bill's new drums and cymbals' clash while I searched the keys around,
Which brought you unexpectedly from your walk along the bay,
Or was our tune alarming which brought you by this way?"

I said, "A combination of the two would more than likely fit,
But since I'm up and hereabout I'd just as soon now sit,
And listen to the passages which accompany the keys,
And have a cup of coffee to sip on, if you please."

So ... with accommodation we four now moved along,
To the music room where Gin and Bill would play and show the song.
I asked, "If I feel comfortable, could I sing along a bit?"
Katrina stretched, then left the room — she'd not be part of it.

Virginia then reminded me, "Bill's music is of ear,
So don't expect a symphony or Berlinish sounds to hear.
We're present for enjoyment, but should you feel the tunes,
Clap your hands and tap your feet or catch the kitchen spoons."

So with Bill on drums and Gin on keys and the cats now far away,
They played the song which Bill had hummed and magnetized "that" day.
There was nothing I could add to the magic present time,
Thus sat transfixed and mesmerized by their rhythm and their rhyme.

Kitty and Katrina ... with knowledge I'd be still,
Marched into the music room as music kitties will.
Their tails in time were waving as batons sent to direct,
With purring and meowing, special sounds they'd interject.

With my applause at music's end, as entertainers do,
Found the Altonberrys bowing, and the cats there bowing too.
　With prompting from yours truly Gin said, "In time I'll write it down,"
And when she does you have my word ... I'll pass the magic 'round!

TOGETHER

    September's orange sea reflects the sun slipping west away,
And hearty laughs heard carry the breadth of Sandwich Bay.
    Recess tugs its mooring lines ... ripples roll away,
No race to win ... just bob about ... as year-long lovers play.

    William raised his ginger ale, the toast his heart proposed,
"Virginia Fairchild, though a year has passed, love within me grows.
    And although I've said it times before, I'm so thankful for the day,
That heaven sent this malcontent a flower 'cross the bay."

    "Now William Altonberry, that's enough of that —
You know it makes me giddy, all your loving 'chitter chat.'
    And though you know I appreciate the sentiments proffered,
The presence of the cats aboard makes me think a cooler word.

    "Yet let me sit and hold the hand that played the capturing tune,
That brought this fading woman a year's-long month of June."
    And she raised the wine glass in her hand, "William, here's to you,
Know the stories of our coming year will be filled with loving too."

    Twilight's breeze fills billowed sail, now *Recess* slips along,
And Virginia spins the coursing wheel while William spins a song.
    The sun is near descended and nighttime's coming on,
The bow is turned to heading home and the cats purr sleeping song....

Bon Voyage....

    Leo Carpenter is a retired special educator (no, not an English teacher!) who taught in Wellesley, Massachusetts. He is a resident of Mexico Beach, Florida and summers on Cape Cod. Leo enjoys motoring on his scooter, pedaling his bicycle and sailing aboard his 22-foot Catalina.

    Born and educated in Massachusetts, Leo is a veteran of the Korean War. He turned his hand to writing poetry because, *"That's the way it came out ... plus my back was stiff and I couldn't build a house. So, I wrote a few poems."*

About the Type

This book was typeset in Maiandra GD, a shapely sans serif font known for its soft, casual charm. The large x-height and almost-serifs instill a sense of warmth to the text, pulling the eye along in an easy, enjoyable manner.

Karmichael Press is located near the beautiful Gulf of Mexico along Florida's *"Forgotten Coast."* Our goal is to produce quality, distinctive books and audio books that readers will be proud to own and keep on their shelves.

We invite you to visit our site on the World Wide Web:
http://www.homtown.com/karmike

Or, for a free catalog featuring our current titles, write:

Karmichael Press
HC 3, Box 155D
Port St. Joe, FL 32456

"Books to enjoy ... and remember!"